O8-CCO-920

The Kentucky Bicentennial Bookshelf
Sponsored by

KENTUCKY HISTORICAL EVENTS CELEBRATION COMMISSION
KENTUCKY FEDERATION OF WOMEN'S CLUBS

and Contributing Sponsors

AMERICAN FEDERAL SAVINGS & LOAN ASSOCIATION
ARMCO STEEL CORPORATION, ASHLAND WORKS
A. ARNOLD & SON TRANSFER & STORAGE CO., INC. / ASHLAND OIL, INC.
BAILEY MINING COMPANY, BYPRO, KENTUCKY / BEGLEY DRUG COMPANY
J. WINSTON COLEMAN, JR. / CONVENIENT INDUSTRIES OF AMERICA, INC.
IN MEMORY OF MR. AND MRS. J. SHERMAN COOPER BY THEIR CHILDREN
CORNING GLASS WORKS FOUNDATION / MRS. CLORA CORRELL
THE COURIER-JOURNAL AND THE LOUISVILLE TIMES
COVINGTON TRUST & BANKING COMPANY
MR. AND MRS. GEORGE P. CROUNSE / GEORGE E. EVANS, JR.
FARMERS BANK & CAPITAL TRUST COMPANY / FISHER-PRICE TOYS, MURRAY
MARY PAULINE FOX, M.D., IN HONOR OF CHLOE GIFFORD
MARY A. HALL, M.D., IN HONOR OF PAT LEE,
JANICE HALL & MARY ANN FAULKNER
OSCAR HORNSBY INC. / OFFICE PRODUCTS DIVISION IBM CORPORATION
JERRY'S RESTAURANTS / ROBERT B. JEWELL
LEE S. JONES / KENTUCKIANA GIRL SCOUT COUNCIL
KENTUCKY BANKERS ASSOCIATION / KENTUCKY COAL ASSOCIATION, INC.
THE KENTUCKY JOCKEY CLUB, INC. / THE LEXINGTON WOMAN'S CLUB
LINCOLN INCOME LIFE INSURANCE COMPANY
LORILLARD A DIVISION OF LOEW'S THEATRES, INC.
METROPOLITAN WOMAN'S CLUB OF LEXINGTON / BETTY HAGGIN MOLLOY
MUTUAL FEDERAL SAVINGS & LOAN ASSOCIATION
NATIONAL INDUSTRIES, INC. / RAND MCNALLY & COMPANY
PHILIP MORRIS, INCORPORATED / MRS. VICTOR SAMS
SHELL OIL COMPANY, LOUISVILLE
SOUTH CENTRAL BELL TELEPHONE COMPANY
SOUTHERN BELLE DAIRY CO. INC.
STANDARD OIL COMPANY (KENTUCKY)
STANDARD PRINTING CO., H. M. KESSLER, PRESIDENT
STATE BANK & TRUST COMPANY, RICHMOND
THOMAS INDUSTRIES INC. / TIP TOP COAL CO., INC.
MARY L. WISS, M.D. / YOUNGER WOMAN'S CLUB OF ST. MATTHEWS

4 2455

92
B
Yan

David Wendel Yandell

Physician of Old Louisville

NANCY DISHER BAIRD

c. 1

Middletown Elementary School
Library

THE UNIVERSITY PRESS OF KENTUCKY

Research for The Kentucky Bicentennial Bookshelf
is assisted by a grant from the
National Endowment for the Humanities.
Views expressed in the Bookshelf do not
necessarily represent those of the Endowment.

Reprinted

ISBN: 0-8131-0245-6

Library of Congress Catalog Card Number: 77-80461

Copyright © 1978 by The University Press of Kentucky

A statewide cooperative scholarly publishing agency
serving Berea College, Centre College of Kentucky,
Eastern Kentucky University, The Filson Club,
Georgetown College, Kentucky Historical Society,
Kentucky State University, Morehead State University,
Murray State University, Northern Kentucky University,
Transylvania University, University of Kentucky,
University of Louisville, and Western Kentucky University.

Editorial and Sales Offices: Lexington, Kentucky 40506

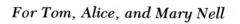

For Tom, Alice, and Mary Nell

Contents

Preface

NINETEENTH-CENTURY physicians enjoyed few of the advantages of their modern brethren, for the practice of medicine usually was neither lucrative nor prestigious, and thus it attracted few cultured, well-educated men. David Yandell was a noteworthy exception. His general education and his medical training exceeded those of most of his contemporaries, and his status as a professor and his efforts to improve medical education set him apart from the majority of his colleagues.

The Yandell name is closely associated with medical education in Kentucky. David's father, Lunsford Pitts Yandell, was a founder of the University of Louisville's medical department, and during his twenty-two-year teaching career at the school it became one of the nation's largest and most outstanding institutions. A scholar of varied interests, Lunsford Yandell produced more than a hundred scientific treatises and edited two medical journals. His three sons followed in his professional footsteps. William, the youngest, moved to the Southwest shortly after receiving his medical degree, but Lunsford, Jr., and David served on the school's faculty and received recognition from their contemporaries as teachers, writers, and editors of distinction. Of the three Yandells who taught at the university, David was the most interesting and most influential, for his outgoing personality, cosmopolitan nature, and longevity propelled him into the prominence denied his more scholarly father and his less aggressive brother.

David Yandell's life centered around the University of Louisville, and his association with it spanned half of the nineteenth century. To the university and its students Yandell gave the benefits of his excellence as a teacher and surgeon, of his progressive ideas on medical education, and of the immense popularity and sterling reputation he enjoyed with other physicians in the United States and Europe. Although he was not a typical doctor of the era, most of the situations he faced as a student, professor, military surgeon, and practicing physician were symptomatic of his times. Typical also were the University of Louisville and its problems, for the nation's medical schools were plagued by financial handicaps, competition for students, feuding faculties, limited curricula, and inadequate teaching aids. This study does not claim to be a definitive study either of Yandell or of the university and medical education, but it hopes to provide the reader with an introduction to all three.

The format of the Bicentennial Bookshelf precludes extensive documentation. The standard works on Kentucky and medical education were consulted, but only direct quotations have been cited. Most of these are found in the letters and diaries that comprise the two collections of Yandell Family Papers at The Filson Club. The larger collection, presented by Malcolm Henderson, a descendant of David's sister, consists of nearly 700 items written before 1870 by David's parents and siblings. The bulk of the smaller collection, a gift from David's great-grandson, W. R. Wood, contains letters written to David by his personal friends and professional admirers; the majority of the physician's personal papers apparently were destroyed, and thus many questions still remain unanswered about his activities and those of his immediate family.

The cooperative efforts of many persons were necessary to complete this study. To the librarians at The Filson Club, the Kornhauser Health Sciences Library at the University of Louisville, the Kentucky Library at Western Kentucky University, the Louisville Free Public Library, and the Louisville Board of Education, I extend my appreciation for aid in locating materials not obvious or readily available. Special thanks are given to James F. Bentley of The Filson Club, Dwayne Cox of the University of Louisville Archives, Dr. D. P. Hall, a former member of the surgical department at the University of Louisville, and W. R. Wood for their interest and suggestions; to Dr. Lowell H. Harrison of Western Kentucky University for his guidance and constructive criticisms during the preparation of the manuscript; and to my husband, a graduate of the University of Louisville School of Medicine, for his explanations of myriads of medical terms.

A research grant from Western Kentucky University made this study possible. The support and encouragement of my family made it a pleasure.

1

THE LOUISVILLE
MEDICAL INSTITUTE

O N MAY 4, 1898, Louisvillians paid final tribute to one of
the city's most distinguished residents. Accompanied by the
tolling bell at City Hall, the friends, professional colleagues,
members of the local chapter of Confederate veterans, and a
regiment of the state militia conducted the remains of Dr.
David Wendel Yandell to Cave Hill Cemetery, where he was
buried on a tree-dotted hillside overlooking a picturesque
lake. Tributes were published in leading newspapers and medical journals across the nation, and his widow received letters
of condolence from men of international fame in Philadelphia,
New York, London, and Edinburgh. With Yandell's death the
medical profession lost an interesting and versatile man and
the most widely esteemed member of a family that had
molded and directed medical education in nineteenth-century
Kentucky.

The first American Yandells immigrated to Pennsylvania
from the British Isles early in the eighteenth century, and
their descendants crossed the mountains from Mecklenburg
County, North Carolina, to Tennessee when the area was still
a wilderness. David's grandfather, Wilson Yandell, was a typical frontier physician, for he was "almost always on horseback,
leaving home before breakfast and seldom returning before
dark" to attend his patients scattered throughout the country-

1

side.[1] In his progeny he apparently instilled an aptitude for science and a strong desire to alleviate suffering, for Wilson Yandell was the first of six generations of physicians. His son Lunsford Pitts Yandell attended Transylvania University in Lexington, received a medical degree from the University of Maryland (then in Baltimore), and returned to Murfreesboro to establish his practice and marry Susan Wendel, daughter of a prosperous local merchant. Their eldest son, David, was born September 4, 1826, and was named for his maternal grandfather.

Shortly after David's birth, Lunsford and his family moved from his father's residence at Craggy Bluff, a beautiful tract of land on the east branch of Tennessee's Stones River, to their own home nearby, and there David experienced the usual delights of early childhood. But rural life confined Lunsford's thirst for knowledge, and in 1830 the family moved to Nashville, where Dr. Yandell enjoyed the company of "scholars" and had access to "rich libraries." In the Tennessee capital David's education began. His mother had planned to teach the boy herself, for that was the custom of the day, but he refused to take her efforts seriously. Hence, the five-year-old was sent to a small private school operated by an elderly couple who exhibited great tenderness to their pupils. David made satisfactory progress; his mother informed a relative that he was "learning his books. He will not be a dunce."[2]

In the autumn of 1831 David's father accepted an appointment as professor of chemistry and pharmacy at Transylvania University in Lexington, Kentucky. Although they were reluctant to leave their home and friends in Tennessee, Lunsford and his wife were aware of the advantages of a professorship. The student fee of $15 per course was paid directly to the teacher, and since Transylvania's medical students numbered more than two hundred a year, the monetary reward for teaching was handsome. Moreover, the position, which involved only a few hours each week during the brief school year, enhanced a doctor's reputation with local patients and private students, who assumed that a professor was more knowledgeable than other practitioners; most faculty members enjoyed a

lucrative practice. There is no evidence to indicate that Lunsford accepted the Transylvania appointment for any goal other
than to distinguish himself as a teacher of chemistry, but the
financial considerations were tempting for a man with a growing family.

After the move to Lexington, David was enrolled at a private school, but within a year his parents became so disenchanted with it that the lad was withdrawn. In a letter to her
father, David's mother reported that during the boy's brief
attendance at the Lexington school he had "retrograded neatly
in pronunciation, had contracted many vulgar expressions,
learned many awkward habits . . . learned little that he ought
to know and a great deal that he could not if we kept him at
home." She also was upset by the teacher's frequent use of
severe punishment, for "no boy was ever made a scholar by
the rod, but many have had the small spark of ambition that
they possessed flogged out of them." Once again Susan
endeavored to supervise David's education and to devote her
time to the "culture of his mind" in order to make sure that his
"growth in knowledge [was] at least as rapid" as his physical
growth.[3] Within three weeks David learned more from his
mother's instruction than he had absorbed in the preceding six
months.

Every morning after breakfast David's lessons began with
"intellectual arithmetic." When he experienced difficulties in
understanding, hickory nuts were used to illustrate the principles of addition and subtraction. After he took a brief rest in
which "his mind sufficiently relaxed," Mrs. Yandell listened to
her son read and then tested his reading comprehension and
spelling. Geography, taught from a book that contained "more
knowledge than our educated men are masters of," was included in the afternoon session. After the evening meal, time
was dedicated to composition and penmanship. David's progress was so satisfactory that his mother believed he would be
able to write a "respectable letter" by his seventh birthday,
and his father approvingly noted that his "temper and manners
as well as his mind" were improving significantly.[4]

Acquiring habits of industry and an interest in physical activities also was part of David's education. Mrs. Yandell expected him to perform chores between his lessons—pack up and carry to the various fireplaces the logs that had been cut, feed his pet pig and the other animals, and do anything else that would eliminate idleness and aid his physical growth and stamina. Dr. Yandell instilled in his son a love of the out-of-doors. He and David enjoyed hunting and fishing (an activity that Lunsford's father called a "scandalous waste of time").[5] They also collected fossils and rock specimens and frequently visited the family farm in Tennessee, where David worked with the "hands." By 1837, when the Yandells moved to Louisville, the eleven-year-old's habits and basic education were firmly established and he was enrolled in a private school. The energies Susan Yandell previously spent in supervising David's education now were consumed in caring for Lunsford, Jr. (called Lunny by his family), who was born in the fall of that year.

The Yandells' move to Louisville was precipitated by a bitter controversy that embroiled the Transylvania faculty and culminated in the founding of a medical school at Louisville. In February 1833 the state legislature had issued a charter to a group of seven Louisville physicians who wished to "promote Medical Science"; the charter named their body the Louisville Medical Institute. No mention was made of a medical school in the charter, but a few years later a committee was appointed to investigate the possibility of creating such a school, and officials at Transylvania were approached about moving their medical department to Louisville, the commonwealth's most rapidly expanding city. Although Lexington's residents and Transylvania's trustees venomously opposed the idea, many of the faculty and students favored it, for Lexington had no hospitals and furnished "very precarious and inadequate means for anatomical study."[6] Late in the autumn of 1836 the school's medical faculty secretly agreed to the move, and by early spring plans were being formulated in Louisville. On March 30 Transylvania Professor Charles Caldwell addressed a group of interested Louisville residents on the advantages of a medical school in their city, and four days later the mayor and his

4

council approved a resolution that made it possible. A square of land bounded by Chestnut, Magazine, Eighth, and Ninth streets was donated for the school and $50,000, to be derived from the sale of twenty acres of the square, was designated to finance the construction and outfitting of the building. Louisville's citizens were so enthusiastic about the medical school that sales of the land brought in nearly $70,000. The land, the institute's future building, and the governing of the school were placed in the care of a Board of Managers, who immediately began to select the faculty. Among the seven chosen were three former Transylvania professors—Lunsford Yandell, Charles Caldwell, and John Esten Cooke.

As plans for the Louisville school progressed during the spring of 1837, relations deteriorated among members of the Transylvania medical faculty and between the cities of Lexington and Louisville. Two members of the faculty, Benjamin Dudley and William Hall Richardson, denied any involvement in the original agreement to move the medical school, but Yandell, Caldwell, and Cooke insisted on their complicity. Accusations were bandied back and forth among them. Dudley accused Caldwell and Yandell of being "guilty of treachery and faithless conduct" toward Transylvania and of encouraging Louisville's "deluded or prostituted press" of trying to ruin the Lexington school. Caldwell and Yandell claimed that Dudley had been the originator of the idea to move the school but that he and Richardson backed out because they were "essentially mercenary and hollow hearted . . . held together by no other tie than that of moral cowardice, like certain ravening but imbecile beasts that prey together."[7]

The controversy also furnished fuel for public feuds, for the towns had long been commercial and political rivals. A Lexington newspaper accused Louisville of trying to "destroy our school . . . [and] injure our city" by luring the medical school and other businesses away from the Bluegrass area. The Louisville press referred to her rival city as a "pastoral village or a declining and decaying town," but denied any desire to steal all of her institutions. "We would not advocate the removal of the Lunatic Asylum. That is appropriately located.

. . . Her present race of statesmen will likely need an asylum in their old age."[8]

The Louisville Medical Institute opened for its first session on October 31, 1837, with eighty students, many of whom previously had attended Transylvania. Temporarily housed in the upper rooms of the City Work House, which was "unattractive, straitened and comfortless," the school boasted a "sufficiently extensive library, apparatus and all the appliances necessary for the illustration of the several topics of instruction." Clinical instruction, a modern innovation not found at most American medical schools, was given at the Marine Hospital, the city's only hospital, opened in 1823 for the benefit of Louisville's indigent residents and the many rivermen who frequented the town. At the hospital students followed their professors through the wards and "observe[d] disease under the direction of experienced and able teachers."[9] Because of the rapid increase in enrollment student visitations to the wards soon became impractical. In 1840 a theater—the first large medical amphitheater in the West—was added to the hospital. Equipped with a skylight, the amphitheater served as the school's major clinical facility, and demonstrations were performed there until the 1880s.

On February 22, 1838, the cornerstone of the magnificent $45,000 medical building, designed by Gideon Shryock in the Greek Revival style, was ceremoniously laid "in the presence of a great concourse of citizens." The three-story brick structure was erected on the southeast corner of College Square, the huge plot of land donated by the city, and was expected to be ready for use by the opening of the 1838 session. Illness among the construction workers delayed completion, however, and only a few rooms were usable when school began. To a colleague in Lexington, Lunsford expressed pride in the handsome building, and when he was "low spirited," he found confidence and hope by "surveying its grand dimensions . . . [and] splendid and graceful proportions."[10]

The interior of the edifice was as practical as it was handsome. A two-story chemical theater, a small chemical room where experiments were prepared and reagents kept, and four dissection rooms occupied the ground floor. The second story contained a large library and a lecture room for classes in pathology, materia medica (pharmacology), and medical theory and practice. The library's original holdings numbered about 1,200 volumes, but in the summer of 1838 Professor Joshua Flint purchased for it $15,000 worth of books and other necessities in Europe; within a decade the library's holdings were increased to 4,000 volumes, many of which were rare, costly, elegantly illustrated, foreign publications. The top floor housed faculty rooms, an anatomical theater where surgery and obstetrics were taught, and a large museum filled with anatomical models, charts, bottled specimens, and fine paintings for "the illustration of the obstetrical lectures."[11] Each lecture room seated 400 persons, and the anatomical theater enjoyed the additional advantage—and disadvantage—of an illuminating but drafty cupola. No dormitory facilities were available. The annual catalog that advertised the school assured potential students that rooms could be obtained at nominal fees with some of the town's first citizens.

The Louisville Medical Institute rapidly achieved a reputation for excellence and drew students from many nearby states. When David entered the school in the fall of 1844, its student body of more than 350 was nearly twice as large as that of any other school west of the Allegheny Mountains.

The youngest member of his class, David was probably better prepared than his fellow students. He had matured in an atmosphere dominated by scholarly pursuits and for a number of years had been his father's medical assistant, an experience that counted as an apprenticeship. His formal training in the private schools of Louisville and during one session at Centre College (which he found repetitive of his earlier work) had rendered him well versed in science, oratory, ancient and contemporary literature, Greek, Latin, French, and German. Most medical schools, including the Louisville Medical Institute, had no entrance requirements, for the nation's secondary schools and colleges did not usually teach those subjects that

7

would be of value in premedical training. Secondary schools concentrated on the liberal arts, and colleges provided classical courses that were considered irrelevant for a medical education. Premedical training was obtained through an apprenticeship to a practicing physician; few medical students attended secondary schools or colleges. Thus, in an era when little more than literacy was expected of those matriculating into medical school, David was a student of considerable promise.

The regular term commenced on the first Monday of November, but the dissection rooms at the institute had opened early in October, and David and his fellow students were encouraged to spend at least several weeks there, learning rudiments of anatomy. Unfortunately, their efforts frequently were hampered, for many of the anatomical subjects were diseased, deformed, or in an advanced state of deterioration. Cadavers, on which half a dozen students hacked away with minimal supervision or instruction, ripened rapidly in the October heat, and thus the young men were forced to complete their study with more haste than efficiency or to postpone their anatomical studies until winter, when the labs were open only at night. Throughout the school term, classes were held daily from early November through February, excluding Sundays, Thanksgiving, three days at Christmas, and Washington's birthday. Tuition expenses included $15 per instructor's ticket admitting the student to all lectures given by the professor during the term, a $10 dissection fee, and a $5 matriculation fee, which gave access to the library and museum. Because of the varying worth of currency issued by state banks, only Kentucky monies were accepted in payment of fees.

As in most medical schools of the period, a faculty of seven professors, whose impressive-sounding titles were changed from time to time, taught a standard curriculum. Students attended classes six hours a day. Three afternoon sessions were devoted to clinical instruction at the hospital, but all other classes were held at the medical school. The same courses, even the same lectures, were given annually, and as two years of study were required for a degree, David's second year was a

8

repeat of the first. He was advised to concentrate in his first year on basic sciences and on the more advanced ones during his last year. A few special lectures were offered during the summer for regular students, apprentices, and even the general public. Attendance at these summer courses was not required, but the information covered might be included in the oral examinations which were conducted at the completion of the two-year program.

The large classrooms were outfitted with blackboards, charts, bottled specimens, and plaster or marble busts of ancient Greek physicians and august scientists of the Middle Ages and Renaissance. Students sat on hard benches or straight-backed wooden chairs, and the professors lectured from a dais at the front of the room. Note-taking was encouraged, but few students recorded more than the basic tenets of each day's lecture. Classroom attire was quite formal. David and his fellow students wore business suits, and the professors appeared before their classes in ruffled shirts and "a great show of collar on their black dress coats."[12] The lecturers to whom David listened included some of the most prominent figures in early-nineteenth-century medicine—Lunsford Pitts Yandell, Charles Wilkins Short, Henry Miller, Jedediah Cobb, Charles Caldwell, Daniel Drake, and Samuel David Gross.

David's father was the school's professor of chemistry. Tall, slender, with a dark complexion and black, penetrating eyes, he was a man of stern and restless disposition, a frequent victim of migraine headaches and melancholy. With his students he enjoyed a remarkable rapport, for he had a kind word for everyone and an uncanny memory for names and faces. Chemistry, as taught by Yandell, was a combination of physics, inorganic chemistry, and natural philosophy. Yandell was extremely interested in the weather and believed that climatic and atmospheric conditions had a bearing on the occurrence of disease. His students were thoroughly instructed in his theory. A man of great versatility, Lunsford Yandell was also a prolific writer, a paleontologist of note, and a serious student of the Bible. He and Daniel Drake edited the widely circulated *Western Journal of Medicine and Surgery*, one of the best examples of early-nineteenth-century medical journalism.

Professor of materia medica and medical botany was Charles Wilkins Short, who was more of a botanist than a physician. His students frequently found his lectures had little or no direct bearing on the use of plants in medicine. Short was an instructive but uninteresting speaker; most of his lectures were read from a manuscript. When he extemporized, he looked over the heads of his students, "fixing his fine blue eyes on some far and elevated point in the room, and, rising and falling on his toes, delivered his carefully prepared prelections." An amiable although modest and shy man, Short apparently was not suited for the turmoil that characterized the medical school. When he received an inheritance from an uncle in 1849, he retired.

With Dr. Henry Miller, David studied obstetrics and diseases of women and children. A native of Glasgow, Kentucky, and a graduate of Transylvania, Miller was a prolific writer, but most of his early published efforts were expended in scathing attacks on physicians with whom he disagreed. Miller was slow in speech, and his lectures at first seemed tedious; but as the session advanced, David became increasingly interested in the subject. It is doubtful that David ever witnessed a delivery during his medical school days, for the social dictates of the era prohibited such "exhibitions." The mechanism of labor was studied from manikins and life-size drawings. Nevertheless, from Miller students heard of the various means of delivering the difficult cases that family members, the usual "obstetricians," were unable to manage.

David's professor of anatomy was New Englander Jedediah Cobb, the school's dean and treasurer. David later wrote that in a "voice clear as a bell," Cobb "stripped the intricate points of anatomy of their obscurity and lodged them in the minds of even the dullest hearer. . . . He had great suavity of manner and was a prime favorite with the students."[13] Cobb was the only one of David's instructors who did not publish, and therefore it is impossible to know the contents of his lectures or the theories he espoused.

The most controversial member of the faculty was professor of clinical medicine and medical jurisprudence, Charles Caldwell. Educated at the University of Pennsylvania, the nation's oldest medical school, he had spent most of his life teaching and writing. During his lectures Caldwell stalked the platform like a caged lion. His students were impressed with his scholarly language, dignified bearing, and interest in a variety of subjects—phrenology, spiritualism, speculative philosophy, history, and religion—all of which he discussed brilliantly; such topics were, however, of little practical advantage to medical students. Years later, David described his former professor as a "massive man in body and mind. . . . His manners, usually cold, were always stately. . . . He was a man of affairs and delighted in controversy. He taught the physiology of the day, which was largely the physiology of the ancients, but he taught it in so impressive a manner that his classes received it as gospel and voted him its greatest expounder."[14]

Caldwell's colleagues were not so flattering in their evaluation of the egotistical professor, who once claimed that the four greatest minds of America included those of Henry Clay, Daniel Webster, and John C. Calhoun; modesty prevented him from naming the fourth. A contemporary noted that if conceit indicated greatness, Caldwell "would have reached the pedestal of fame," and most of his associates commented on his refusal to keep abreast of new ideas.[15]

Daniel Drake, professor of pathology and the practice of medicine, was probably the best known of the faculty members, and as a lecturer he had few equals. His words were full of vitality, his eloquence fervid, and his manner earnest and impressive. Drake's daily lectures contained moral advice as well as scientific information. He urged the young men to draw their pleasures from the "discovery of truth" and their amusements from the "beauties and wonders of nature" rather than from debaucheries. To gain knowledge, Drake confided, "a man must observe; to get understanding, he must think."

Lest his students become more interested in medicine as a business than as a profession, Drake constantly stressed that the foundation of a good medical practice was "laid in the hearts of the poor. . . . The poor will be the most grateful of all your patients. Lend a willing ear to all their calls." The importance of clinical records and thorough autopsies was another of Drake's favorite themes, for from them a doctor would increase his knowledge concerning disease and erase the "clouds of false doctrine and error" which prevented proper treatment of many cases.[16]

Of all his professors, David was most influenced by Samuel David Gross, professor of surgery. In the decade before his move to Louisville, Gross had published two monumental works on anatomy and surgery and with them won national acclaim. A sometimes excited, even boisterous lecturer, who looked his students in the eye, shook his fist, stamped his foot, and swore "by the Eternal" to impress his point upon their minds, Gross was a rigid disciplinarian but a superb instructor. Astute at applying principles to the practice of surgery, he "infused interest into the dryest details of his subject" and made "every case illustrate some principle of surgery [and] descended to the minutest detail of bedside practice." His course was divided into general and special surgery, with considerable time spent on "inflammation and its consequences of tumors and morbid growths," the different kinds of wounds, and general principles of surgery.[17] The second segment of the course concerned injuries and diseases of particular tissues, organs, and regions of the body. Special attention was given to fractures and dislocations. All surgical demonstrations were performed on cadavers; students learned by watching, and their first attempts at operating would be on their own private patients, away from the guidance of the experienced instructor.

Operating with great dexterity and skill, Gross was a fanatic on the topic of cleanliness and believed that some yet unknown pathogen, transmitted by the surgeon's hands or instruments, caused the infections that were responsible for the high mortality rate among surgical cases. His theory was not generally accepted by his colleagues. While other surgeons emphasized speed, Gross stressed cleanliness. Gross also impressed David with the necessity of being receptive to new ideas. During the early 1840s surgery was in an embryonic state. The use of anesthesia and the discovery of effective antiseptics were still in the future, and thus surgery was a harrowing and dangerous ordeal. Gross would be one of the first physicians in Kentucky to appreciate the use of ether and chloroform during operations. Until the introduction of antiseptics in the late 1870s, personal cleanliness would be the only means of preventing infection.

No records have been found of David's daily activities during his medical school days, but one of his classmates, Henry Clay Lewis, published a delightful sketch of his own experiences at the Louisville Medical Institute. Lewis claimed that the typical first-year medical student was devoted to everything but his studies. He was habitually late to class, his notebook was filled with caricatures of his professors rather than with lecture notes, his evenings were spent in carousing instead of studying, his money was taken by gamblers instead of booksellers, and his energies were consumed with such pranks as substituting dissection room specimens for the pot roast on the boardinghouse table. Consequently, the "first termer" was a frequent inhabitant of the city jail and in constant danger of expulsion. During his second year, however, a student endeavored to do everything possible to impress his professors with his knowledge, for he was a candidate for a degree.

David may have been sufficiently well supervised by his parents to prevent his participation in such dissipations, but he was not a model student. Among his classmates he was known for his oratorical talents and his scholastic laziness. Perhaps it was immaturity that caused the lad to exhibit more interest in preparing and delivering addresses to the school's medical society than in studying his books. His classmates were puzzled at his ability to answer questions in class correctly without "closer appreciation to his studies" and concluded that "by some means [he] obtained knowledge intuitively."[18] Not awed by his knowledge, David's professors hesitated to graduate him with his class in March 1846. Graduation requirements were carefully stated. A candidate for a degree had to complete two years of apprenticeship to a practicing physician and two years of classes at the institute, write an acceptable thesis, pass the oral examinations that were conducted by the faculty, be twenty-one years of age and of good moral character, and pay a $25 graduation fee. Since the withholding of a degree affected each teacher's income, few candidates were denied a diploma.

The reason for the faculty's reluctance to permit David to graduate is unknown. He had met the stipulations concerning the apprenticeship and class work and had written a thesis on hematology, but there was the question of his minority of age—the age requirement frequently was waived, however—and the examination. The oral questioning required for graduation was a frightening experience. Lewis compared it to having swallowed poison with "no stomach pump about, or slept with a man with smallpox . . . or shaken hands with the itch" and described the examiners as "seven old dried up specimens of humanity who looked as if they had descended for the occasion from some anatomical museum and who have looked upon death, suffering and the annual ranks of medical aspirants" until their hearts were as hard as stone. The examination period was appropriately dubbed the "Ides of March."[19] Questioned privately by each professor for fifteen minutes, the student was supposed to receive an intense grilling on the instructor's subject, and if more than three of the seven faculty members held doubts about the candidate's competency, he was refused a diploma. David later claimed that if there was any hesitancy to graduate him, it did not stem from the examination. He wrote that Daniel Drake lauded his answers as among the "best in all his experience as an examiner," that Cobb told him that he "passed a beautiful examination in anatomy," and that Gross loudly professed his excellence.[20] Lunsford's evaluation of his son's performance is unknown. Nevertheless, it was rumored that someone re-marked that David was a "damned unpromising specimen," and this comment was remembered long after the words of praise were forgotten.[21]

An embarrassing situation was prevented when the faculty learned that David's education would continue with post-graduate studies in Europe. For the remainder of his life there would be speculation by his enemies that the promise of addi-tional schooling, "the Grace of God and the good will of the faculty" were the only reasons the professors agreed to bestow an M.D. degree on David Yandell.[22]

2

THE "DAMNED UNPROMISING SPECIMEN"

Early in the spring of 1846 the University of Louisville was created by the state legislature. An eleven-man Board of Trustees, appointed by the mayor and his council, was to manage the affairs of the university's three departments—medicine, law, and academics. The law department opened in the fall of 1846. The university's "Academical Department" did not materialize until 1907, but its building, which was erected in the late 1840s at Ninth and Chestnut, was used briefly by the law department and then became the home of Louisville Male High School. The Louisville Medical Institute was incorporated as the university's medical department, but the transaction was only a legal form. The faculty continued to elect their own officers, choose new professors (whom the trustees automatically approved), collect student fees, and assess themselves when funds were needed for repairs and improvements on their building. In reality the medical school remained autonomous; only its name was changed. At the opening of the 1846–1847 session Dr. Caldwell announced: "In obedience to the decree which controls the fate of all that is sublunary, the Medical Institute of Louisville is no more; its brief but splendid (I had almost said glorious) career was forever closed. . . . At the same moment, on its site and out of its relics was erected the Medical Department of the University of Louisville."[1]

David was not present to hear his former professor deliver the institute's funeral discourse. Two weeks after his graduation the nineteen-year-old boarded the steamboat *Ben Franklin* and began a lengthy trip that culminated in two years of postgraduate studies at the medical centers of London and Paris. His recorded observations and experiences, many of which were published in the *Louisville Journal* and the *Western Journal of Medicine and Surgery*, reveal a cocky but impressionable lad who was compassionate, observant, articulate, and witty.

David's journey to New York was highlighted by brief visits to several cities along the way. Following an eight-hour trip upriver, he spent a weekend in Cincinnati. He boarded at the Broadway Hotel, which was found wanting because the grate in his small room was insufficient to "invite one to sit before and toast his shins," and toured some of the Queen City's points of interest—Nicholas Longworth's garden, the observatory on Mount Adams, and Saint Philomena Church, the "most imposing work of catholicism I have yet seen."[2] Unable to locate a Presbyterian church, David attended Sabbath services at Christ Episcopal Church on Fourth Street. At the conclusion of the service he waited at the door to notice and be noticed by some of Cincinnati's lovely young ladies. His effort was in vain. He saw none that could compare to Louisville's belles in beauty and charm.

From Cincinnati Yandell went by boat to Pittsburgh and then traveled overland to Baltimore, Washington, and New York. In Baltimore he visited his father's alma mater and was the guest of Chief Justice and Mrs. Roger B. Taney. Always appreciative of pulchritude, David was more impressed with Taney's daughters and with the other young girls he met in Baltimore than he was with the prestige of his host or with the school from which his father had received a medical degree. David was cordially accepted by everyone he met and concluded that the Baltimoreans "possessed far more of southern hospitality than I had supposed." In the nation's capital his host was the United States congressman from Jefferson County, Kentucky, William P. Thompson. The young doctor's brief visit to Washington was filled with touring public buildings, meeting political leaders of note, and visiting with the "President and Presidentess," the James K. Polks, who were distantly related to the Yandells.[3] After a brief stay in Philadelphia, David lodged with Lewis Sayre in New York. Sayre, one of Lunsford's former students at Transylvania, introduced the Kentuckian to numerous physicians of prominence, several of whom became David's lifelong friends.

Amply supplied with letters of introduction from his friends and recent acquaintances, David embarked on the three-week trip across the Atlantic. His passage to Liverpool aboard the H.M.S. *Ashburton* cost $100 and was marred only by the loss of his overcoat, "stolen by some scamp." Among his fellow passengers were the Belgian minister to the United States and numerous lovely ladies with whom David apparently spent many enjoyable hours. Confiding in his diary, he wrote that he could not "travel with comfort or pleasure without ladies. I must have them. . . . Miss Wilkinson is pretty and no doubt ready for a flirtation, Mrs. Jackson to talk sense to, Miss H——to talk about home to, etc. I anticipate a pleasant voyage."[4]

David arrived in London early in May, four months before his twentieth birthday. He visited many historic sites and enjoyed observing the English people at work and play, but most of his time was spent in the lecture rooms and hospitals connected with London University Medical College. Only a few lectures were given during the summer months, for the main school year extended from October to April. Nevertheless, the student body during the summer session numbered more than a hundred.

The curriculum at the school was not rigidly defined, and students chose the subjects they preferred. The $20 to $40 fee charged for each course was paid directly to the instructor. Additional fees of $75 per annum were required for access to the various university-associated hospitals. Despite this expense, the students who watched renowned physicians operate and who crowded around the beds of patients to hear "the master diagnose and prescribe" were so numerous that Yandell complained he "saw disease but could neither feel nor hear disease."[5] Fees also were required for admission to university libraries, museums, and dissecting rooms. Anatomical specimens were purchased by students at rates Yandell deemed outrageous.

Advanced students could obtain practical experience in medicine and surgery by purchasing, for $150 to $250, appointments as house surgeons, clinical clerks, and dressers (surgical assistants who performed duties similar to those of modern surgical nurses and recovery room attendants). Although David disapproved of selling positions rather than awarding them on merit and of charging extra fees for what he believed should be part of every student's curriculum, he readily approved and quickly adopted the English custom of copious note-taking in small, bound notebooks. The Kentuckian also found that the classroom chairs, to which were attached planks that served as writing desks, were an excellent invention, and he suggested that his father's lecture room be equipped with similar devices.

Earnest, energetic, assiduous, distant, indifferent, and selfish were the adjectives David used to describe his fellow students who were neither as "intelligent looking" nor as "fine in appearance" as the young men with whom he had graduated a few months earlier. Yandell expressed surprise at the lack of intimacy between colleagues. Students of the same class frequently remained unacquainted throughout the term, and, unless formal introductions had been made, they would not speak to one another but would "stand right up before you and look most ludicrously frigid."[6] The same isolation apparently prevailed among the faculty members and between faculty and students. Many students who had made hospital rounds with a professor for three or four years had neither spoken to the teacher nor been addressed by him, and several outstanding members of the faculty were unacquainted with one another.

An exception to the lack of intercourse between students and teachers, one which troubled the Kentuckian, was the

19

manner in which the surgeons talked to their dressers. If bandages were awkwardly applied, ulcers improperly cleansed, or instructions not followed implicitly, the dresser would be accused publicly of stupidity, incompetence, and lack of dedication. Yandell recognized the need for cleanliness and good nursing care, but he also appreciated the advantage of tactful, constructive criticism. American students, he asserted, would not tolerate such rude attacks on their egos.

Although he described most of the lecturing professors as "feeble of voice" and "extremely dull" in their presentation, Yandell acknowledged their expertise. The young physician's favorite professor was Sir Robert Liston, an eccentric and energetic professor of clinical surgery, who seemed to "perceive by intuition the nature of disease and the remedy for it."[7] Yandell watched several of Liston's operations and was impressed by his deft and precise handling of the knife, the meticulous care with which he sutured and bandaged incisions, the detailed and comprehendible instructions he gave for postoperative care, and his operating attire—a *clean* coat instead of the traditional soiled apron worn over street clothes.

David had intended to stay in London until Christmas, 1846, but he discovered that few opportunities were available to him during the summer months, when most of the professors were vacationing. He journeyed to Belfast in July for a brief visit and in mid-August left the British Isles for Paris. He had enjoyed the first leg of his European adventures and hoped that during his brief stay in London he had succeeded in correcting John Bull's misconception that Americans were "bowie knife carrying men" and "thin lipped, sallow complexioned women" who spawned few men of note and that the English were the "most gifted, best educated and bravest" people in the world.[8] Years later, during the height of his career, David would return to the British Isles and discover that both he and the empire had become more tolerant and appreciative of each other.

A diligent medical student "scorns delight and lives laborious days," and Yandell's schedule during his two years in Paris was a busy one.[9] He dressed and breakfasted by candlelight each morning and at eight joined the students from the École de Médecine to make hospital rounds with the medical and surgical faculty. Classes, which commenced at midmorning, were held in amphitheaters and large lecture rooms outfitted with hard benches. The number of students frequently exceeded the available seats, and the scramble for places to sit resulted in a great deal of chicanery and rowdy behavior. Nevertheless, Yandell was impressed by the general politeness and friendliness of French students but was dismayed that so few of them were able to take notes because of the lack of elbow room and desk facilities.

Many of the École's faculty members were highly acclaimed in the United States, and David acknowledged his good fortune in being able to attend their lectures. Unlike the English physicians, the Parisian faculty members were interesting, often eloquent, lecturers, and their subject matter frequently was more advanced, with greater emphasis on anatomy, than Yandell had encountered in Louisville and London.

The three topics discussed in the classroom and hospital wards that most interested Yandell were the use of sulfuric ether as an anesthetic, the prevention of infections (especially erysipelas) in hospital patients, and the treatment of syphilis. While the last was a subject that had challenged doctors throughout the ages, the others were relatively new fields in which the Parisian physicians pioneered. Surgical anesthesia had received limited use and an abundance of criticism in the United States since its introduction in the early 1840s. The Parisian faculty not only advocated the use of anesthetics but also experimented with the best manner of administering them and with the safest and most effective dosage for different types of surgery. Yandell and several students anesthetized each other and found that the inhaled ether produced a pleasant sensation. Since it calmed the patient, prevented pain, and lessened operating-room tension, the young physician concluded that, properly used, anesthesia was a blessing for both the patient and the doctor.

Experimentation in the use of chemicals to prevent and cure

infections and skin eruptions that plagued hospital patients and increased the mortality rate also excited the Kentuckian. Unfortunately, effective antiseptics were unknown, but David was cognizant of the need for something more potent than soap and water to control deadly pathogens, and he studied intently the results of the various preparations advocated by the French doctors.

Hospital and clinical facilities in Paris exceeded anything Yandell had previously known. Small groups of students were assigned to various faculty members at the city's ten public hospitals, and in these limited groups a student had the opportunity to study each patient, examine him thoroughly, and follow his progress from admittance to dismissal, or in fatal cases through a complete autopsy. According to David, an industrious student in Paris could see in one morning the cases of both the medical and surgical wards, hear a clinical lecture, and be present at the postmortem examinations. "And if he be strong and fleet of limb he may follow Roux through his wards at the *Hotel Dieu*, Jobert through his at *St. Louis* and hear Velpeau lecture at *La Charité*." [10]

Additional instructions were also available for $5 per month at private clinics, many of which specialized in particular areas, such as dermatology (which included venereal disease), ophthalmology, and otology. Yandell's spare moments must have been filled with private instructions, for he assured his father that "by embracing the opportunities which these men afford . . . the student will learn most." [11] He carefully recorded for his father's journal the various medical and surgical procedures and diagnostic and therapeutic treatments that he witnessed.

The use of *internes* was a French contribution to medical education. Medical school graduates who wished to gain more extensive experience competed for openings on hospital staffs where they managed the clinical facilities, acted as assistants to the master surgeons, and frequently gave private instructions to beginning medical students. David was impressed with the contributions these men made to the administration of the hospitals and the care of the patients. The use of such postgraduate students would be one of Yandell's innovations in Louisville's hospital system.

The cost of a medical education in Paris was considerably less than in London. The school's museums, libraries, and anatomical facilities were free to the graduates of any medical school as well as to the École's students. David commented that for less than half the price of a London cadaver, Parisian students could purchase a corpse, receive instructions in anatomy and dissection, and "have their knives regularly sharpened in the bargain."[12]

Shortly after the close of the 1847–1848 winter term, David bid Paris adieu. He attended a medical congress in Vienna, briefly visited several French, German, and Dutch cities of historic interest, and returned to Louisville in the summer of 1848 to practice his profession. Although he was less than twenty-two years old, he boasted a medical education that few American doctors could equal. He had studied with some of the most eminent men of the scientific world and had witnessed, treated, and written about a great variety of maladies. The residents of Louisville who read his letters in the *Louisville Journal* were impressed with the knowledge they believed he possessed, and colleagues who followed David's series of articles in the *Western Journal of Medicine and Surgery* profited from and perhaps were envious of his experiences. His writings were quoted and praised in various medical periodicals. The most flattering review, written by the eminent Dr. Oliver Wendell Holmes of Boston, was read to the delegates of the 1848 American Medical Association Convention at Baltimore. For many years David would be remembered for his enlightening letters and his sprightly writing style.

On his return to Louisville the "unpromising specimen" of two years earlier joined his father in the practice of medicine. Within a few months his reputation as a physician was well established. His medications probably were no more successful than those of his colleagues, but his patience, charm, and dedication gave him the appearance of being more knowledgeable than most of the town's other physicians. Unfortunately, success went to his young head, and his inflated feeling of self-importance nearly involved him in a duel and indirectly caused the death of a friend.

The incident resulted from a disparaging remark made about the young doctor by a Dudley Hayden. David retaliated, and accusations and sharp words were conveyed between the men by local busybodies. To protect his honor and good name Hayden dispatched a note to Yandell. Learning that the physician was likely to appear on the field of honor, a group of his friends met with Hayden and his second at the Galt House and convinced Hayden that an apology was preferable to a duel. During the celebration that followed the successful negotiations, several of the diplomats became inebriated, and a fight broke out between Henry Clay Pope and John Thompson Gray. The badly bruised Pope challenged Gray to a duel, and in the resulting confrontation Pope was fatally wounded. Yandell undoubtedly felt some moral responsibility for the death of his childhood friend, but dueling was an accepted, if illegal, means of settling disputes between gentlemen, and the unfortunate affair seems not to have harmed David's professional reputation or social standing.

In the fall of 1849 David accepted an appointment at the university as clinical assistant. In this capacity he supervised the dissection labs, assisted Professors Elisha Bartlett and Samuel Gross, and procured anatomical specimens for their classes and for the lab. Despite his busy medical practice and laboratory responsibilities, Yandell found time to instruct apprentices. The standard apprenticeship, through which most American doctors received all of their medical training, usually ran for two years. The preceptor furnished all the books and equipment and instructed the student on all he should know; for his services he received $100. The apprentice "read" medicine, performed simple chores for the doctor, accompanied him on house calls, and occasionally assisted him in treating his patients. Only a small portion of apprentices continued their education at a medical school; and since any practitioner could be a preceptor, the student's education was only as thorough as his master's knowledge, instructive ability, and sense of responsibility. Many apprentices did little more than care for the doctor's horses, sweep out his office, and concoct his medicines, but Yandell's students were said to have received as excellent training as was available in the Midwest.

One of the major problems faced by eager young apprentices was the lack of a practical method of studying anatomy and surgical techniques. To aid their apprentices—and anyone else who desired the instruction—Yandell and Dr. Robert James Breckinridge, a member of the university's faculty, established a dissection laboratory on Jefferson Street and there conducted private classes in anatomy, physical diagnosis, and surgery. Little is known about the short-lived facility, but apparently it was operated as a small school offering the advantages of a dissection lab and daily demonstrations and lectures. Yandell's effectiveness as a teacher attracted attention and increased his fortune.

Late in the summer of 1850 Gross and Bartlett resigned their chairs at the university, and the faculty began to contemplate the problem of replacing them. Several members of the faculty wished to offer the positions to men whose well-established reputations would increase the school's educational standing and enrollment; others wanted to bestow the appointments on friends whose fortunes and reputations would be enhanced by faculty status. Local doctors, who resented competition from outsiders, pressured the teachers to choose the new members from physicians already practicing in Louisville. To the resigning professors and several other faculty members, including his father, David Yandell seemed the most obvious candidate for one of the vacated positions. There was, however, opposition to his youth.

During the several weeks of faculty feuding that preceded the final decision, the young physician appeared unconcerned and visited with the family of a Nashville belle. His father, who remained in Louisville, worried enough about the appointment for the two of them. To his wife vacationing at Murfreesboro, Lunsford wrote a letter warning her against being too confident of the appointment. David's chances probably would be better if he were a married man, he wrote, but David had "twice the reputation Gross had when he came here and can be made as great a man in a year." Pouring out his hopes and fears, Lunsford speculated that David's friends were "astir" and that the number of his advocates was growing. However, as it became increasingly apparent that sentiments were strong for men of greater reputation and maturity, Lunsford comforted himself with the realization that "even if he misses his mark, he wins by aiming high. Very soon he will be obligated to come in." Lunsford suggested that they leave the decision in "the hands of Providence." Nevertheless he complained because some of his colleagues objected to having a father and son on the faculty simultaneously.[13]

Despite his father's wishes, David was not the majority's favorite, and in an effort to preserve departmental harmony Lunsford cast his vote for Dr. Paul Eve of Nashville for the surgical chair and for Dr. Daniel Drake, who had been in Cincinnati the preceding four years, for Bartlett's former post. The faculty minutes do not reveal the opinions expressed against David's candidacy, but it appears that resistance to a father-son combination was an important factor. Numerous vacancies occurred from time to time, but David was not again seriously considered for the faculty until his father retired from it in 1859.

Though disappointed at not obtaining the university chair, David found solace in Nashville. In April 1851 he married a well-to-do Nashville beauty, Frances Jane Crutcher. For almost a year David had visited the Crutcher home with regularity and kept his parents guessing as to which of the Crutcher girls, Fanny or her younger sister Elizabeth, he favored. Well-acquainted with the Crutchers, who were distant cousins, Lunsford secretly favored Elizabeth, but he admitted that Fanny was the "more amiable—that is perfectly amiable." When David announced his marriage plans, his parents were pleased, for they believed that the "cares and demands of a family stimulate a man as nothing else will." Susan's heart was won at "first sight" by her future daughter-in-law's "quiet sweetness"; Fanny was a "lovely girl both in mind and manners," a "real treasure." Lunny paid Fanny her greatest compliment several years later when he announced that he wanted to find a wife like "Sister."[14]

After the wedding the young couple returned to Louisville and "no girl ever left Nashville so much regretted." A former beau expressed the sentiments of Fanny's Nashville friends when he lamented that David was the "destroyer of my happiness."[15] Just before their marriage David had purchased a home on Walnut Street, but it is doubtful that the newly-weds ever lived in it. A few months after their wedding they moved to Woodlawn, Fanny's farm a few miles from Nashville, and David expressed his intent to engage in agriculture. The reason given for the sudden change in address and vocation was David's "poor health," but the cause of the young physician's decline was never mentioned. Fanny might have been homesick, but it is improbable that David would have abandoned his home and lucrative practice to appease a feminine whim. It is more likely that he believed his career was suffering in the shadow of his father's reputation and hoped that he might be asked to join the faculty of the Nashville Medical School. His mother warned him against giving up a profitable practice to go to a town that was one-fourth as large and "one-tenth as enterprising" as Louisville. With Gross gone, she contended, David could soon command all of the surgical practice in Louisville; it was better to be a first-rate practitioner in Louisville than part of a "third or fourth rate school" in Nashville. Lunsford hoped that whatever his son decided, he would "find peace through belief. There is no reason why he should remain out while there is so much room in the House of our Heavenly Father."[16]

David ignored the advice given by his mother, and it is doubtful that he realized the religious fervor that his father enjoyed and wished for him. This brief residence in Tennessee was the halcyon period of his life. He supervised operation of the farm, hunted and fished whenever possible, practiced his profession, honeymooned with his young bride, and celebrated the birth of his two eldest children, Maria and Allison, his only son. Blessed by the benefits of country air and the affections of his growing family, David's "health" improved

27

rapidly, and late in the fall of 1854 he and Fanny returned to Louisville. They moved into his father's new home on Chestnut Street near the medical school, and David rebuilt his practice. Within the next half-decade his professional activities, fortune, and family responsibilities increased immensely. He became the proud father of two more daughters, Susan and Martha, wrote numerous articles for midwestern medical journals, acted as preceptor for many young apprentices, including his two younger brothers, became active in state and national medical societies, and joined with other Louisville physicians in setting up a scale of fees for professional services.

A couple of years after his return from Tennessee, David opened a free outpatient clinic on Fourth Street near Chestnut. Named for the Irish physician William Stokes, benefactor of Dublin's poor, and modeled after the private clinics in Paris, Stokes Dispensary was financed with fees paid by medical apprentices and university students, who enrolled to gain additional knowledge and practical experience. At the daily sessions Yandell supervised the students as they diagnosed and treated the city's indigents, who flocked to the first such clinic in the West; patients with unusual maladies served as demonstration subjects and were cared for by Yandell. The physician kept detailed records of the cases treated at his clinic and hoped to publish them. Subscriptions for the proposed report were taken, but no copies of it have been found. All records of the dispensary have disappeared and thus nothing is known about the manner in which it was conducted. Nevertheless, the facility received the praise of physicians who toured it during a state medical conclave in Louisville, and since it supplemented rather than competed with the university's offerings, the medical faculty lauded Yandell's innovative teaching.

The success of Yandell's dispensary was due, in part, to the university's financial problems. A small portion of the matriculation and graduation fee was retained for maintenance and repairs on the buildings, but funds for additional facilities had to come from the pockets of faculty members, who were careful not to approve projects that would be expensive. Building, outfitting, and operating a dispensary required considerable outlay of money—more than the faculty was willing to spend. In 1850 the Kentucky School of Medicine had been founded in Louisville, and competition for students and their tuition fees became keen. Rather than increase its expenses or tuition, the university urged students to use David's clinic.

The institution's financial burdens were compounded on December 31, 1856, when a faulty stove caused the medical building to burn to the ground with the loss of all the contents except for a portion of the library's holdings. Insured for two-thirds of its value, the school was rebuilt on a plan similar to that of the original building and was financed with private loans from its faculty members with assistance from the university's trustees. When the new building opened, the faculty invited David to teach clinical anatomy classes there on Saturday evenings. For his services he received the student fees, excluding a small sum to cover expenses for heat and lights. The faculty also asked him to edit a medical journal that would advertise the school, but when the estimated printing costs of the proposed project were received, this idea was abandoned.

In May 1859 the university played host to the annual meeting of the American Medical Association. The delegates' praises were heaped on David Yandell, who had reluctantly taken over the planning of the convention at the last minute because the faculty members either refused or were ill equipped to plan and carry out a well-executed affair. The daily work sessions of the AMA meetings were preplanned by the association's officers, but the host organization was responsible for the entertainment that followed each day's business. David prevailed upon friends, including the James Trabues and the Robert J. Wards, to open their palatial homes to the organization. Their formal receptions, which were attended by the elite of Louisville as well as by the delegates, were dazzling affairs. The closing banquet was given at the Wards' mansion, and David planned and supervised every detail of it. An advocate of moderation, he intended that the affair should not become a drunken row. After sufficient liquor had been served to the guests, David locked the closet where it was kept; per-

29

sons who insisted on more were referred to the Galt House, a well-known Louisville hotel. During the latter part of the evening, he discovered that a young waiter had secreted for himself a private supply of intoxicants. When David requested that the lad return the bottles, the sassy youth told his unknown challenger that only Dr. Yandell could tell him what to do. Sternly, David identified himself and informed the young man, "If you don't put them down, I'll beat this bottle over your head and hand you over to the police." The young man did as he was advised and the evening's festivities were not marred.[17]

Throughout the four-day meeting Susan Yandell delighted in the compliments that were paid to her eldest son. Many of the delegates were surprised to learn that despite his reputed professional excellence and obvious administrative abilities and talents as a writer and speaker, David was not a member of the university faculty. Mrs. Yandell predicted that David would benefit from the AMA meeting more than anyone else, for he was "by far the most efficient of the Louisville doctors."[18]

A few weeks after the meeting Lunsford Yandell resigned his chair at the Louisville institute, and the faculty resolved that David "be recommended to the Trustees to occupy the chair of Clinical Medicine and Pathological Anatomy."[19] David's ascension to faculty status was the realization of a decade-long ambition, but as in the case of many diligently pursued goals, its acquisition resulted in less than the expected pleasure. Disputes with other professors over the management of his clinic, which had been absorbed by the university shortly after he joined it, vexed him. His major contribution appeared in the school's new bylaws. As head of the rules committee, David insisted that provisions be made for the creation of three postgraduate positions similar to those held by French *internes*, to be awarded to the school's top graduates after a rigorous, competitive examination. Unfortunately the Civil War prevented the new program from being put into effect.

Although David's struggle to obtain a professorship was

30

hampered by his father's position, his younger brother Lunny found Lunsford's fame an asset and achieved a faculty appointment with little effort. An 1857 graduate of the University of Louisville's medical school, Lunny wanted to continue his studies in Europe. The Yandells believed that "no sacrifice is too great for our children," and that the slow-to-mature Lunny would benefit emotionally as well as professionally from additional experience. Unfortunately, decreasing enrollment at the university since 1850, poor collections for his medical services, and overextension in his real estate investments kept Lunsford hard pressed for money. Thus Lunny practiced medicine in Louisville for two years, but in the spring of 1859 he moved to Memphis, the most rapidly growing city of the West. His brief residency there was marred by frequent bouts of illness, homesickness, and financial worries, and he concluded that Memphis "won't do to live in."[20] His appointment to the Memphis Medical College in the summer of 1860 provided the only bright spot in his two years in the river town.

Founded in the mid-1840s, the Memphis Medical College had never achieved the success enjoyed by the school in Louisville. By the late 1850s a miracle was needed to prevent its demise, and Lunny's father was approached by several members of the faculty to help save the school. With his influence, they reasoned, Lunsford Yandell could "write the professors into famous reputation and the school into prosperity hitherto unknown in the annals of medical schools." Hoping that such a move would solve his pressing financial problems and give his middle son's career the boost it needed, Lunsford resigned from the University of Louisville and agreed to aid the Memphis college and "have one more grand fight before I die."[21]

Under Yandell's supervision the school was reorganized, and Lunny received an appointment as professor of materia medica, a position for which the twenty-three-year-old felt inadequately prepared. David bolstered his brother's spirits and appearance for his new responsibility by sending him several exquisitely tailored jackets and occasional monetary gifts.

The preparation of class lectures was an educational experience for Lunny, and at the close of the 1860–1861 session he admitted that the previous winter had been one of the most satisfactory of his life. Their new positions might have been financially rewarding for Lunsford and his namesake had war not broken out that spring, bringing ruin to the Memphis Medical College as to numerous other medical schools in the South.

Susan Yandell remained in Louisville while her husband and son were in Memphis, but in May of 1860 she journeyed south to visit with her men. Deaf and suffering from a chronic kidney infection, she was weakened by the trip, and shortly after her arrival in Memphis she was stricken with typhoid fever. Despite the expert care provided by her husband and son, the disease proved fatal. To the four of her thirteen children who survived infancy, she had been a wise "guide and counsellor." On the eve of his own death, Lunsford acknowledged that to Susan he owed his success: "She kept me steady and to my purpose. She made me what I am."[22]

Typhoid visited David's household later that summer. David survived, although he was in bed for several months, but one-year-old Martha did not. One cannot but grieve for Fanny, who, while mourning for the mother-in-law she adored, buried her baby and cared for her three lively children and her desperately ill husband. A loving, conscientious, shy woman, she also had to assume some of the responsibility for David's now motherless younger brother and sister, who lived with them part of the time Lunsford was in Memphis. Because they were so much younger—Willie was born the year David entered medical school and Sally arrived while he was studying in Europe—David seemed more like an extra parent than a brother. Sally apparently resented his and Fanny's authority and complained that her sister-in-law showed marked preference for her own children and that David was "crotchety." She was assured that although David might scold her, "he will always do it for your own good."[23] In the spring of 1861 Lunsford remarried and shortly thereafter Sally moved to West Tennessee to be with her father.

David's youngest brother, Willie, was the best natured member of the family and enjoyed a carefree boyhood in the bustling city of Louisville. During his eighth and ninth summers Willie kept a diary in which he recorded the important events of his day. Young boys can identify with this contemporary of Tom Sawyer who "rose early and washed all over. . . . have been pretty good—didn't fret sister much—cried once."[24] Living only one block from the medical school, when he was a little older he frequently provided transportation from the railway depot and steamboat wharf to the medical school for students arriving in the autumn and gave visitors a tour of the medical building. He chauffeured his mother, Fanny, and their friends around town, and, when alone, drove the family wagon at death-defying speeds on the back roads. Willie was seventeen when his mother died. The following winter he lived with his father in Memphis and attended the medical school. Despite his youth his academic progress was quite satisfactory, but the climate aggravated his asthma. Thus, Willie returned to the Falls City early in the spring of 1861 to study as David's apprentice. He planned to enter medical school in Louisville the following winter, but his plans, like those of the other men of his family, were changed by national events. The armed conflict that erupted in the summer of 1861 altered the course of their lives.

3

MEDICAL DIRECTOR

When the university's medical faculty met on September 20 to discuss arrangements for the opening of the 1861–1862 session, Louisville was bustling with military activity. Kentucky's five months of neutrality were over, and everywhere could be seen the blue uniforms of Union soldiers. The seemingly unsolvable sectional conflict that had dominated the nation's politics and emotions for more than a half-century had erupted into a civil war that placed the commonwealth in an unenviable position.

A border state, Kentucky was linked socially, politically, and economically with both North and South. Many of her citizens harbored strong states' rights sentiments or were sympathetic with relatives who lived in secessionist areas. Although her slave labor system was that of the southern states, Kentucky's commercial interests depended on both sections—perhaps more strongly on the North. Strategically important to the antagonists was Kentucky's control of the confluence of the Ohio and Mississippi rivers, a vital north-south invasion and supply route. In hopes of preventing the state from becoming a battleground for the belligerents, Kentucky had claimed neutrality, an artificial and impossible position that melted away in the warm, rainy days of September. Confederate forces moved into the Columbus area September 3, and the Federals advanced to Paducah the following day. By mid-September northern portions of the state were under

Union control and a Confederate army was gathering at Bowling Green. Armed conflict on Kentucky soil seemed imminent.

Even while the state was officially neutral, its citizens did not remain aloof from the nation's volatile situation, and throughout the summer and fall of 1861 Kentuckians of all ages declared their loyalties. Many families were divided and furnished soldiers for both sides. The Yandells, however, were of one accord. Lunsford supported the preservation of the Union until April 1861, but when President Lincoln called for troops after the bombardment of Fort Sumter, Lunsford cast his lot with the Confederacy, for he feared that Lincoln was a "monster willing to plunge his country into civil war and wreak his vengeance on the South."[1] By the end of the summer the senior Yandell's greatest concern was the immediate safety of his family. Willie had run off to join the Confederates training at Camp Boone near the Tennessee-Kentucky border, and Lunny, an ardent secessionist who said he would "despise" himself if he did not volunteer in the defense of the South, enlisted as a private so that he could advance his reputation and experience "excitement and . . . glory." But when his commander suggested to him that "one of your name naturally belongs to the medical department," Lunny reluctantly accepted a commission as a surgeon.[2] His martial spirit was quickly squelched when he witnessed the horrifying death and suffering of his fellow man. Lunny served the wounded at Columbus, and after the Confederate defeat in southwestern Kentucky he joined General William J. Hardee's forces at Corinth and served with the tactician as surgeon and medical inspector for the remainder of the war.

Unlike so many of the South's physicians who enlisted as fighting men and later accepted commissions as military surgeons when the need for them became acute, David Yandell applied for and was immediately granted a commission in the Confederate medical department. His sympathies for the Confederate cause were known to his family and colleagues by midsummer, and it is therefore unlikely that his resignation from the faculty and his commission came as a surprise. At the

September 20 meeting of the faculty, the dean read David's letter expressing his "unallayed regret" at resigning from the school. He promised, however, that "should times change, and with that change I return to Louisville, I shall always be ready to afford the institution from which I now so reluctantly withdraw, my very heartiest, though it be feeble, support." Leaving his medical equipment, laboratory specimens, and "any monies coming to me" in the university's care, he had "abandoned" the family home in Louisville, which Lunsford predicted would be "confiscated by the tyrant in Washington."[3] The doctor and his family had departed in early September for Nashville, and Fanny and the children began a five-month visit with Fanny's sister Elizabeth, now Mrs. George Maney. By the time his letter of resignation was read to the faculty, David was in Bowling Green with General Simon Bolivar Buckner's forces.

Whether David joined the Confederate army because of strong political sentiments, loyalty to his native Tennessee, desire for fame, or a combination of all these is unknown. Regardless of his motives, his acquaintances viewed Yandell as the epitome of a southern gentleman and military Galahad. His tall, slim body, ruddy complexion, brown eyes, and chestnut locks were enhanced by his bearing and manners and by his sonorous voice and magnificent command of the English language. Dressed in the medical officers' uniform (a cadet gray tunic accented with black facings and gold star on the collar, dark blue trousers striped with black velvet edged in gold, sash of green silk net, white gloves, black cravat, black Jefferson boots, and a gray cap on which the gold letters M. S. were embroidered), David Yandell must have cut a handsome figure at the officers' dances and parties, when his official duties allowed time for such frivolities.

During his first weeks as surgeon in the Provisional Army of the Confederate States, Yandell made numerous trips between Bowling Green and Nashville to supervise the supplying of Buckner's forces with medical necessities.[4] He enjoyed his duties and association with Buckner, who had been a neighbor in Louisville, but because the general believed that

Yandell's administrative abilities fitted him for greater responsibilities, the physician was assigned in mid-October to General Albert Sidney Johnston, commander of the Army of the West. A few weeks thereafter, Johnston elevated his surgeon to the greatest field responsibility in the western medical department—the medical directorship of the Army of the West.

The jurisdiction of the Army of the West encompassed an area that extended from the Appalachian Mountains to Indian Territory, but most of the army's 48,000 troops were in southern Kentucky. As medical director of this military monstrosity Yandell administered the medical affairs of the entire army. The task would have been a difficult one for a man with many years of military experience and adequate resources; it was a gargantuan job for the former civilian doctor. The army was plagued with epidemic diseases; medicines and supplies were nearly impossible to secure; hospital facilities were inadequate; and most physicians and nurses were, at best, poorly trained and inexperienced.

Many of the troops that arrived in Kentucky during the fall of 1861 were from Mississippi and southern Tennessee, unaccustomed to and unprepared for the rigors of a Kentucky winter. The majority of them were from rural homes and had never been exposed to the highly contagious diseases now generally experienced by school children. Thus they were highly susceptible to a variety of maladies that were caused or complicated by lack of proper clothing and bedding, by exposure to the elements during that year of a rainy autumn and severe December temperatures, and by contaminated water and poorly prepared foods. Rampant epidemics among the closely confined men all but incapacitated the Army of the West.

Throughout late November and December one-half of the command at Dripping Springs had measles and scurvy, three-fourths of the forces at Oakland were felled by measles and pneumonia, and only one-half of the troops at Columbus were able to stand for roll call. The commander at Hopkinsville reported in late October that so many of his soldiers were ill or engaged in nursing duty that "I am not more than able to patrol the town."[5] Throughout the fall and winter smallpox, measles, dysentery, typhoid, and influenza visited the encampments at Bowling Green, and similar epidemics prevailed at the Mississippi River forts and eastern Kentucky camps. The need for hospital facilities was immediate.

At Bowling Green, a town of about 2,500 inhabitants, Yandell planned to create a centralized treatment center for the army, but existing facilities were extremely limited. There were no hospitals and very few large public buildings, and the hotels and boardinghouses were filled with the soldiers' dependents who had accompanied them to war. Yandell's efforts to convert the Green River Tavern into a 100-bed hospital were temporarily frustrated by the money-hungry proprietress, who agreed to rent the building for $50 per month to the army only if it purchased the hotel's furnishings for $2,500. Since most of the furniture was unsuitable for hospital use, the doctor suggested that accommodations for 250 men should be erected and outfitted by the Confederate government, an idea that received approval from the surgeon general's office. But the incidence and severity of illnesses increased more rapidly than building projects could be finished, and Yandell was forced to accept the hotel owner's proposal and to make additional arrangements for the sick men. At Hopkinsville a large tobacco stemmery and the homes vacated by persons fleeing the war zone were used for infirmaries. Yandell also created a small hospital at Russellville. The Shakers at South Union were requested to provide immediate care for several hundred men, but they had accommodations for only a dozen or so. In desperation David secured for several days the services of 80 enlisted men to enlarge Camp Recovery, a tent city on the eastern edge of Bowling Green. He also commandeered public and private buildings, which were topped with a yellow flag to denote their hospital use. By late November more than 1,500 men were receiving care in Bowling Green's makeshift infirmaries; the number increased as the weather became more severe. Willie was among those treated for camp fever at Bowling Green. When his six-month enlistment was up,

David obtained a discharge for him and urged the lad to go to Memphis and make use of his medical knowledge by helping their father care for the sick in that city.

Despite Yandell's efforts ministrations to the sick were inadequate. A volunteer nurse who managed a hospital in Bowling Green was shocked by the great suffering, which was compounded by "want of organization, lack of suitable buildings, [and] scarcity of supplies."[6] The diary of a young Union sympathizer in Bowling Green provides a pathetic account of the soldiers' plight as the winter of 1861–1862 came on.

December 3rd
It is cold and sleety and a sad sight we saw as we came from town this evening. Bob Strange's Cooper Shop has been taken for a hospital and as we passed there we had to wait to let soldiers bring out to the wagon the body of a young fellow who had just died, with measles which ran into pneumonia a soldier told us and whilst we waited it was pitiful to hear the poor fellows in the hospital coughing and to see the pale and forlorn looking men who were regarded able to be up and think how little of needed care they could have in such conditions.[7]

While men languished in makeshift hospitals, an unidentified number of the luckier ones received care in private homes throughout the town, where clean bedding, home-cooked meals, and constant attention were provided. Placing sick soldiers with local families apparently created difficulties for Yandell's post surgeon at Bowling Green. Unable to keep up with who was where, he inserted a notice in the newspaper requesting all residents who were caring for his charges to submit the names, ranks, and regiments of their patients.

Although he intended to make Bowling Green the army's main treatment center, Yandell planned to establish in Nashville a hospital for convalescents and the chronically ill. There too the doctor was confronted with problems. Following several "fruitless days" of searching, he obtained three storehouses that, after repairs and refitting, accommodated several hundred men. Yandell also anticipated using the State Hospital until he discovered that a group of physicians had leased it for a medical school. The faculty offered to provide free care for the Confederate soldiers, but Yandell, who was well acquainted with the abilities and potentials of many Kentucky and Tennessee physicians, questioned their administrative expertise for such an undertaking. Rather than adopt the Tennessee governor's advice that the Confederates should occupy the State Hospital by force, Yandell tactfully recommended a change in the staff. Dr. Paul Eve, a former teacher at the University of Louisville medical department, whom Yandell labeled "the leading surgeon of the south," a man whose presence would "secure for the medical department the increased confidence in the profession," accepted a commission in the Confederate medical department and was appointed director of the hospital. The former head was commissioned and received the command of a small field hospital, where his experiences and abilities were expanded rather than overwhelmed.[8]

The Tennessee legislature made provisions that aided Yandell's efforts. Nashville's Blind Asylum was set aside as a temporary hospital, and the Clarksville Female Academy received permission to "rent, give or lease the Academy buildings and grounds" for the sick. Unfortunately, these were insufficient to meet the demands. Yandell was forced to set up thirteen hospitals in Nashville and to seize homes and businesses "whose owners positively refuse to rent for the need I require." By early November 800 soldiers were "properly lodged and comfortably provided for" in Nashville, and additional hospitals had been created in Murfreesboro, Columbia, Franklin, and Memphis.[9] During the five-month encampment in Kentucky, more than 4,000 Confederates were sent to the convalescent centers in Nashville for extended care. The casualties from the engagements in western Kentucky would be taken to Memphis and the other Tennessee hospital sites.

The problems of procuring hospital space were compounded by travel arrangements to Nashville. Patients whose recuperation would be lengthy and the overflow from the Bowling Green hospitals were transferred in freight trains. Passenger trains might have provided greater comfort, but they arrived in Nashville after dark, a confusing time to receive sick men. Since it was not economically feasible to provide special daily trains just for the transportation of the ill, and because the hospital staffs were too small to accommodate the occasional arrival of large groups, the regularly scheduled freight service was used. A similar schedule was used for those returning to Bowling Green. The travel accommodations, though convenient for the medical personnel, were frightening for the passengers. A young soldier who was sent to Nashville by boxcar later wrote that the trip from Bowling Green was "the dreariest ride" of his life, for he was "alone, in the darkness, suffering excruciating pain, [perhaps] going to die and be buried in an unhonored grave." [10]

The inability of his subordinates to estimate correctly the number of beds needed in Nashville hospitals further complicated Yandell's work. The medical director was supposed to be notified, eighteen to twenty-four hours in advance of their arrival, of the number of men being sent. Unfortunately, the anticipated and the actual numbers frequently differed and arrival times were often miscalculated. Thus nurses, food, ambulances, and beds awaiting the expected patients were sometimes wasted, and others who needed the prepared facilities were denied them. Several of Yandell's dispatches to surgeons in Bowling Green were sharp in their criticism of the procedures of doctors who did not properly supervise the embarkation or provide the required number of nurses to care for the men en route.

It appears that some of the men transferred to Nashville were suffering from disillusionment with military life rather than from illness, for Yandell requested that guards be stationed on the convalescent trains. He informed General Johnston that there were many soldiers in Nashville "who have escaped from the hospital and others who have in some way managed to escape from the 'sick trains,' who cannot be gathered together and shipped to camp except by force," a commodity not available in Nashville. Yandell was dismayed to learn that during one week in January at least twelve men had deserted and eluded detection. [11]

41

Acquiring enough doctors and nurses was a task that consumed much of Yandell's time and energy. The *Regulations of the Confederate Medical Department* specified one surgeon for each small hospital or one surgeon and assistant surgeon per 75–80 men in larger ones. Yandell considered the number insufficient and staffed his hospitals with more physicians than the directive allowed. When extra medical personnel were needed, he employed civilians. The Kentuckian received numerous reprimands from the surgeon general's office for contracting too many local doctors and at salaries above the allotted amount. The "contract doctors" complained because they were hired as assistant surgeons rather than surgeons, who commanded better pay and enjoyed greater prestige.

Although much of the nursing care was provided by female volunteers (such as Ella Newsom, who brought five servants and a carload of supplies from her home in Arkansas to Bowling Green in December 1861), Yandell was forced to recruit additional help from the ranks and from local civilians, including unemployed "free negroes who at present are of no service to themselves or our country." On numerous occasions Yandell commandeered the services of slaves, despite the objections of their masters, who were compensated, nevertheless, for their servants' labors. The allocated pay for a civilian nurse was $30 a month, but Yandell believed that for $40 a higher grade of attendant, who could provide better care for more patients, could be acquired. Similar difficulties were experienced in hiring competent hospital cooks and stewards. To his commander the Kentuckian expressed the hope that "in a very short time it will be possible to hire both cooks and nurses at a much smaller figure. . . . The militia law will drive a good many men to the hospitals for employment in order to avoid enlistment."[12]

Quality and quantity of personnel were always a problem. Yandell tried to pick the best man for every job, and most of his recommendations for commissions and appointments were honored. As the talents of his subordinates expanded with experience, Yandell advanced them to positions of greater responsibility. In providing regimental surgeons, however, he met difficulties. It was the custom for enlisted men to choose their regimental officers, including the regimental surgeons, and "good fellows" rather than competent officers were frequently selected. Attempting to remedy part of the grievous situation, Yandell suggested that all medical appointments pass through his hands. Unfortunately, it soon became apparent that no one person could know the qualifications of every man who claimed to have medical knowledge. After hearing "frequent complaint[s] of the incompetency of many of the surgeons," the Kentuckian urged that a board of medical examiners be established to screen all medical department applicants. His suggestion was accepted.[13]

The examining board, on which Yandell served as president, set up minimum standards and tested the knowledge of all applicants for commissions and contracts with the army's medical department. Recommendations for commissions were granted only for medical school graduates whose examinations were judged "creditable." A nongraduate with knowledge sufficient to entrust "the lives of our soldiers to his hands" could be placed under contract as an assistant surgeon. The examinations were oral and were harrowing experiences for eager, although nervous, doctors. On one occasion the victim of Yandell's intense grilling about gunshot wounds brightened when asked what he would do for a "shot right through there," the medical director pointing to his own knee. "Well, Sir, if it was you that was shot through there, I would not do a d——d thing," announced the applicant with reckless revenge.[14]

Yandell also established a board to review all applicants for medical discharges. The board consisted of the medical director and several surgeons and met twice a week to consider all requests. It is doubtful that the group kept records of their examinations, but they received sufficient discharge requests to necessitate the creation of separate boards for Nashville and Bowling Green.

As medical director of the Army of the West, Yandell believed that he "made a name" for himself that "nothing that any military man could do would seriously affect."[15] He took his responsibilities seriously and expected his subordinates to do likewise. He was a stern taskmaster, demanding that surgeons and their assistants examine and prescribe for each patient daily and remain at their posts at all times rather than "loitering about the streets and otherwise absenting themselves from the hospital" or "lounging about the Post Hospital and in the drug store." Yandell warned that "if they be fitted to exercise their art upon sick soldiers, they will find occupation for their whole time in keeping their books, studying their cases and watching the interest and comfort of the inmates of their wards." [16] All surgeons were required to submit monthly reports to the medical director, and those that were filled with errors were returned to their authors with mild reprimands. Late reports also caused consternation, and on one occasion Yandell expressed resignation at ever receiving any kind of report from several of his surgeons.

Despite his assiduous efforts to provide good medical facilities for the thousands of ailing soldiers in Johnston's army, there were complaints about the fruits of Yandell's labors. Local pharmacists objected when their drug supplies were confiscated or purchased with inflated money; volunteer nurses were irritated because physicians treated them in a condescending manner; and generals groaned when their ranks were thinned for nursing details. The soldiers, whose illusions about the glamour of the military were quickly dimmed by camp life, complained about everything—and there was plenty about which to complain! Even in the most severe weather many of Johnston's men had only one blanket, an inadequate covering in the unheated tents and mud-and-stick huts in which they lived. Many men were without overcoats and heavy shoes. Beds for the temporary hospital facilities and for the men's quarters usually were made from a board covered with a thin layer of straw and a blanket; the memoirs of one soldier noted that straw was so scarce in Bowling Green that there were only "seven straws to nine men." [17] Hospital food was often unappetizing and lacked the nourishment that sick men needed to aid them in regaining their strength. Although few medicines were known that could have combated effectively the illnesses that rampaged, all medical supplies were difficult to obtain in great quantities. The various communicable diseases were not segregated. Patients recuperating from one malady were likely to contract another contagious disease, and the combined illnesses frequently were fatal. The exact number of sick and dead is unknown. An undertaker in Bowling Green, where the most severe cases were treated, later estimated that he furnished 3,000 coffins for the Confederates. Others believed that more than 1,000 were buried in the Bowling Green area while an undetermined number were returned to their families for interment. Whatever the count, the losses were high.

Apparently there was only one formal complaint lodged against Yandell's endeavors. In mid-December a Dr. Barnett claimed that the "accommodations and administrations" of the Bowling Green and Nashville hospitals were "not of a character to recommend them to the favor of the sick men and others." Bristling with indignation, Yandell answered Barnett's "grave charges" with an offer to discuss the complaint with him and investigate and correct the matter if the charge was substantiated. As to Barnett's accusation that the mortality in Nashville hospitals was unreasonable, Yandell noted that the percentage of deaths was "small to a degree which reflects credit to the skill, attention, management and care of their medical officers . . . who have exhibited heroism and industry. . . . I should not fear to have the bills of mortality in the hospital alluded to compared to those of others in the Confederacy." [18]

In mid-February of 1862 the Confederate forces withdrew from southcentral Kentucky. The retreat to Nashville was precipitated by the unsuccessful endeavors of the Confederates in the eastern and western portions of the state and the advance into Central Kentucky of Union troops led by General Don Carlos Buell. Johnston's plans to stand at Nashville were changed after the Confederate loss of Fort Donelson in western Kentucky, and on February 16 his forces began to withdraw to Corinth in northcentral Mississippi. Yandell had been advised in early February to secure hospital facilities in towns south of Nashville—as far south as Corinth—and to make provisions for the transfer of the hospital inmates at Bowling Green. The evacuation of the sick began several days before Johnston's army commenced its march to Nashville. Five hundred of the ill and 3,500 convalescents who were too weak to endure the march were transferred by rail. Provisions for the 4,000 men had been secured previously, and they were efficiently dispersed to the awaiting facilities. What had not been anticipated, however, was that hundreds of men would become ill during their march to Nashville in the freezing rain and snow. An estimated one-third of Johnston's army needed some sort of medical care upon arrival in the Tennessee capital; 1,400 required hospitalization. Yandell's medical report of February 18 commended his staff for the orderly evacuation of Bowling Green's hospitals and the care given 5,400 soldiers who were rapidly accommodated in Nashville's hospitals.

Throughout February and March, Yandell was occupied with securing, supplying, and staffing hospitals in the Corinth area. Valuable medical stores had been abandoned in Bowling Green and Nashville by the retreating army, but medicines, bedding, surgical instruments, and other necessities were purchased and otherwise secured for Johnston's army. Aided by the mild temperatures of Mississippi's springtime, the health of the Army of the West improved. The small town's supplies were limited, but according to one of the nurses, Corinth "was heaven in comparison to Bowling Green"— heaven until April 6 and 7, when more than 7,000 men wounded on the battlefield at nearby Shiloh were returned to the town to tax its resources and the skills and endurance of its people.[19]

The Battle of Shiloh was one of the bloodiest of the war. Although the medical director's duties generally precluded participation in the actual care of the sick and wounded, David Yandell worked diligently on the battlefield at Shiloh and in the hospitals at Corinth. He had attended an infinite variety of wounds, infections, and diseases during his fifteen years as a practicing physician, but nothing could have prepared him for the carnage he witnessed at Shiloh—gaping wounds, missing limbs, mangled bodies. With no systematic method of retrieving the wounded during battle, hundreds of men bled to death where they fell, and others lay for hours in the blood-splattered mud until found by a comrade or by a detail sent at the end of the day to collect the wounded and bury the dead.

First aid and emergency surgery were administered at hastily improvised field hospitals. Few buildings were near the battlefield, but they and most of the tents that belonged to the Confederates were devoted to hospital use. Care received at these facilities was crude indeed. First-aid packets for battlefield use were unknown; the niggardly supplies of emergency medical necessities and surgical tools were carried by the physicians in their small medical bags. The same instruments were used on one patient after another with nothing more than an occasional rinsing to remove dried blood and tissue. Antiseptics were unknown, painkillers (brandy and opium) were scarce and used sparingly, and the supply of anesthetics was insufficient for the demand. Wounds were probed with unwashed fingers, and bandages were devised from whatever fabric was available. The usual emergency treatment for severe wounds of the extremities was amputation, for the neat cut of a surgeon's instrument was less likely to become gangrenous than was a dirt-filled, jagged wound created by a projectile. The horror of the battlefield was compounded, therefore, by the grisly sight of mounds of arms and legs outside the field hospital tent, where the degree of a surgeon's skill frequently was measured by the rapidity with which he severed the limb. The death rate from shock and infection was much higher than was the rate of recovery.

After cursory attention at the field hospital, the wounded were loaded into ambulance wagons and other available vehicles, and through a quagmire created by the heavy rainfall they were transported to Corinth. Nearly every building in the small town was turned into a hospital. Men lay on floors "so close together that it is almost impossible to walk without stepping on them," and the "foul air from this mass of human beings" sickened many of the attendants. On their arrival at the hospital, volunteer nurses gave the men coffee and bread

47

to revive their strength and replaced their mud-caked, blood-soaked clothing with clean garments. Despite the efforts of the physicians and nurses, gangrene, tetanus, and a host of other infections killed hundreds of men who had survived the enemy's bullets.[20]

Seventeen hundred Confederates died during the two-day battle at Shiloh; Albert Sidney Johnston was one of them. Yandell had been at his commander's side on the first morning so that he could witness "a battle—a big battle." Coming upon the second line of the enemy's tents, they discovered a large number of unattended wounded men. Since no other surgeon was in sight, Johnston insisted that Yandell "look after these wounded people, the Yankees among the rest."[21] Yandell sent a courier to the rear for medical officers, but when Johnston rode on to supervise and direct the battle, his medical director still was attending the wounded men. Shortly thereafter a spent minié ball struck the general just below the knee, tearing without severing the popliteal artery. Within fifteen minutes Johnston bled to death. Earlier, in an unprecedented move, Yandell had issued tourniquets to all of Johnston's staff officers, and the lifesaving device was in Johnston's pocket. Had it been applied above the leg wound, the general's life might have been saved.

With Johnston's death Yandell lost not only his commander and friend but also his coveted position in the Confederate medical department. A few weeks before Shiloh, the Army of the West had been joined by troops from the Deep South, and the combined forces were renamed the Army of the Mississippi. General P. G. T. Beauregard of Louisiana was appointed as Johnston's replacement, and Beauregard's physician, Andrew J. Foard, became the army's medical director.

David remained at Corinth until late April of 1862, when he was appointed medical director of Hardee's corps and president of the Army of Tennessee's Board of Medical Examiners. Both he and Lunny were with Hardee when the Army of Tennessee, under the command of General Braxton Bragg, moved to Chattanooga to prepare for the invasion of Kentucky. Their northward thrust began late in August 1862.

Traveling through a countryside plentiful with ripened fruits and vegetables, the invasion force was optimistic about its goal—to win Kentucky and thousands of recruits for the Confederate cause. Among the army's many supply wagons were several ambulances carrying medical necessities, including demijohns of medicinal whiskey for which the younger officers frequently found personal use. On September 14 the army met enemy forces at Munfordville, and after a brief encounter the Federals surrendered to the numerically superior Confederates. While details of the capitulation were worked out, Yandell and several of his surgeons inventoried and confiscated the Union's medical supplies stored in the town.

From Munfordville, Bragg's army moved into Central Kentucky. General Edmund Kirby Smith's army was also in the Bluegrass area, but neither Confederate commander made any effort to cooperate with the other. Had the two armies combined their energies, they might have made good Bragg's earlier boast that he would be governor of Ohio by mid-October. However, after making little effort to engage the enemy, part of Bragg's army met Federal troops at Perryville. The brief encounter was claimed as a victory by both North and South, but neither side gained from the battle. One-fifth of the Confederates were killed or wounded, and the battlefield was covered with dead men, dead horses, and all the accouterments of war. The 2,600 wounded were taken to hospital facilities in the Harrodsburg area. For two days and nights Yandell and other doctors worked without food or sleep, operating and dressing wounds. When Bragg's army retreated several days later, most of the severely wounded were, by necessity, surrendered to the Federals.

A few days after the Perryville encounter, Bragg admitted that his invasion of Kentucky had been a failure. Union forces still controlled the commonwealth, and the recruits acquired during the swing through the state had not equaled the army's losses, much less its expectations. Thus in mid-October the Confederates began their long march to Cumberland Gap. Hardee, his staff, and a cavalry escort retreated ahead of the rest of the army. Short of supplies and afraid to tarry lest they be caught by the enemy, the advance group slept with "saddles for pillows, arms handy and our horses picketed right at hand—slept with both eyes open." Despite their shortage of food, Yandell enjoyed at least one hot, tasty meal during the retreat. Near Crab Orchard the hungry men spied a lean old ewe grazing on a hillside. Yandell's cook, a Louisville chef of note who had been with the surgeon throughout the war, "bought, borrowed, begged or stole . . . mostly the latter" the ewe. That evening Yandell and his traveling companions dined on roasted mutton and fresh mushrooms, a "feast for ye tired soldiers." [22]

The army's retreat from Kentucky set off scathing criticism against Bragg: many Kentucky soldiers and others believed he lacked the courage to fight. Yandell labeled the abortive invasion "Bragg's terrible blunder." Shortly after the retreat the doctor wrote to William Preston Johnston, aide to Jefferson Davis, and urged his friend to "come out and gather the leading facts & opinions of the Kentucky campaign" and report them to the president. Having seen orders and heard opinions "such as are not vouchsafed to every doctor," Yandell concluded that Braxton Bragg was "either stark mad or utterly incompetent . . . ignorant of both the fundamental principles and the details of his noble profession." Apparently carried away with his recently acquired military expertise, Yandell also offered the opinion that "old greybeard" General Leonidas Polk, who was with them on the invasion, could "do more service on a chronic court of inquiry than in command of troops" and concluded that if "Bragg isn't removed & Polk transferred to house duties, we will all go to the devil out here. Providence alone saved us in Ky. & that in spite of the commander." [23]

Yandell's complaint was not the only one voiced against Bragg, and in December 1862 President Davis visited the general's army. Although there is no evidence to indicate that the commander-in-chief read Yandell's caustic letter, the doctor believed that his plea to Johnston had been responsible for Davis's visit.

Bragg's army was also visited in December 1862 by Kentucky's colorful raider John Hunt Morgan. During his brief visit Morgan married his Murfreesboro sweetheart, and the nuptial festivities were attended by many of Bragg's officers, including Yandell. Well known among the officers for doing imitations of them, Yandell was requested to entertain. During the doctor's "unrivaled impersonation" of General Hardee, which the tactician found very amusing, General Bragg was called from the room and Yandell was cajoled to do his rendition of the gruff old general. Assured that Bragg would be absent for more than an hour, Yandell yielded to the request. "All realized that nothing could be more true to life than his impersonation of Bragg in one of his paroxysms of tigerish ire and expatiating on his favorite themes, of the too prevalent use of whiskey and lack of discipline in the army; striding to and fro, rasping like an Afrite, and jerking out brief sentences in abrupt, raucous utterances."[24]

At the climax of the performance, when Yandell's back was to the door, Bragg reappeared. A "grin of malicious amusement crossed his stern features," and the audience "gave way to the unrestrained laughter," which encouraged the unwary physician to "exert himself all the more strenuously." When he turned around and saw the "grim old martinet," the act abruptly ended. Despite Bragg's insistence that the "entertaining and doubtlessly quite accurate" performance continue, Yandell's efforts were not repeated.[25]

Yandell remained with Hardee throughout the winter and early spring of 1863, serving as his personal physician and friend, and he was commended by Hardee for his "good management of the sick and wounded" at the battle of Murfreesboro, where the casualties were "rapidly removed from the field and cared for before midnight."[26] Early in May of 1863 Yandell was sent to Jackson, Mississippi, to "watch over" the health of General Joseph E. Johnston, and at the general's request the assignment was made official. During the Mississippi campaign that summer, the two men shared quarters and the physician frequently aided Johnston by reading aloud his dispatches and writing the replies the general dictated.

On June 17 Yandell wrote a detailed letter to his successor as medical director of Hardee's corps in which he discussed Johnston's health, energetic activities, and strategy to aid the forces of General John Pemberton, entrenched at Vicksburg. Using lengthy quotations from official dispatches and other correspondence to which he should not have been made privy, Yandell explained and analyzed the cause of the sad state of affairs in Mississippi that could only culminate in the destruction of Vicksburg and the loss of Pemberton's army. The epistle's style and form suggested that it was intended for the public.

Shortly after the July 4 surrender of Vicksburg, criticism of Johnston swelled. His supporters found convenient use for Yandell's letter, for it lauded Johnston and placed the blame for Vicksburg's ultimate fall on lack of cooperation from officials at Richmond and on the refusal of Pemberton to act upon Johnston's suggestions. Numerous newspapers of the South published parts of the doctor's letter, and when President Davis read excerpts from it in the Charleston and Atlanta papers, he demanded to know and was told who had written such a "laudation" of Johnston and "detraction of others." Davis, sensitive to criticism, interpreted the letter as demoralizing to the public and offensive to his administration. The matter was referred to the secretary of war, and Yandell was instructed to explain his actions. Denying that the letter was intended for publication, Yandell insisted then and later that it had been written only as a simple narrative "to inform a friend of current events. . . . Its design was not to criticize; its purpose was not to censure," for he had "no end to gain by the one, no feeling to gratify by the other." Johnston defended Yandell's access to his private papers, but the Confederate president considered the doctor's meddling unforgivable. In November of 1863 Yandell was "banished" to the Trans-Mississippi because of his "highly military offense . . . and also to remove him from that position to one in which he would have less opportunity for exercising undue influence on the army and community."[27]

The physician's sudden departure for Louisiana astonished

52

his friends, who viewed him as a "victim of petty tyrrany [*sic*]." Many of them "offered to unite in a petition to the war department that the order . . . might be revoked," but Yandell refused to permit it.[28] The immediacy of his transfer prevented him from making suitable arrangements for his family, who were staying with friends in Marion, Alabama. The next spring Fanny requested a safe-conduct permit from Joe Johnston, who advised her to write and ask permission from Federal authorities to pass through their lines. Apparently permission was granted, for Fanny and her three children returned to Louisville sometime in the late months of 1864. Their experiences in the Confederate states had been unnerving. While the Army of the West was in southern Kentucky, Fanny and the children had lived at the home of Fanny's brother-in-law, General George Maney, near Nashville. David had urged her to stay with Sally and his father in West Tennessee, but Fanny was "rather timid" about being that close to the Mississippi River, for she had heard predictions of atrocities by the advancing Federals and other "pronouncements . . . calculated to frighten all the women, old men and children." When Bowling Green and Nashville were evacuated, David had sent his family to stay with relatives in southern Tennessee; en route their train derailed at Stones River, but they were uninjured. As the Union army penetrated the South, Fanny and the children took refuge with friends, moving from one farm or plantation to another. The children enjoyed living in the country, "hunting eggs and going into the fields with the hands," but after David's transfer to the West, they longed for home and the relative serenity offered by Louisville. Fanny's family praised her as a noble and heroic woman, but she probably thought of her residency in the Confederate States as a nightmarish experience.[29]

Three months after Yandell was transferred to Louisiana, Edmund Kirby Smith assumed command of the Army of the Trans-Mississippi, and one of his first official acts was to appoint Yandell his medical director. When Lunny heard of his brother's banishment and subsequent promotion, he gleefully wrote his father that David was as "irrepressible as a cat; you can't throw him on his back—He lights on his feet every time, and the harder he is rubbed the brighter he shines. His popularity is universal."[30] Shortly after Yandell's appointment the western forces were involved in fighting along the Red River. Despite the brief time Yandell had to organize his medical staff, it functioned with relative efficiency, and the Kentuckian was commended for "speedily perfecting arrangements for the proper care of the wounded" at Pleasant Hill and Jenkins Ferry. A few days after the Pleasant Hill battle, Yandell met with a Union physician to discuss the care of wounded prisoners-of-war. The surgeon complimented Yandell on his efforts in behalf of the Federal casualties and noted that as physicians their differences were "not so great after all. We are human beings of the same great family with many sympathies in common."[31]

Shortly after the Red River campaign a physician attached to the Department of Texas requested information from the medical department concerning Yandell's authority. Believing the Kentuckian to be his junior in rank, the Texan desired to "be informed if I am expected to report to him and be under his direction."[32] The request rekindled ire in Richmond, for it brought to the attention of the administration Yandell's important appointment in the Trans-Mississippi and suggested that the medical director was exerting authority over men not officially subordinate to him. Despite reports from his commander and the governor of Louisiana concerning Yandell's commendable service during the Red River campaign, Kirby Smith was ordered to remove Yandell as medical director and replace him with any surgeon of his choice. In his unsuccessful defense of Yandell, Kirby Smith chided the Confederate Medical Departments:

The Dept. in directing him to report to me for duty should have informed me of the circumstances under which he was sent to this command and the disposition they desired made of his services. Surgn. Yandell came to this dept. with letters highly flattering to himself from many of the General Officers in the Army of Tenn. With his recommendations, rank and reputation for professional and administrative ability, it is natural that I should have selected him. . . . It is just to Surgn. Yandell and myself to state that in the many months of intercourse as a member of my military family, and messing at the same table I have ever heard him speak in high terms of the President and in support of his administration.[33]

Yandell's sister, who heard from unofficial sources of the demotion, indignantly noted that it was "lamentable to think that the President should be actuated by such petty malice." Yandell's reaction is unknown, but apparently he had long since become disenchanted with military affairs. Shortly after the Red River campaign he confided to a friend that he had ceased to allow himself to worry over problems created by the shortcomings and blunders of the military. "I am well nigh as indifferent to those committed by others, if not those brought home to myself, as a granite sphinx is known to be to a clap of thunder. . . . My *aplomb* is splendid. I only lose it now as a consequence of too much whiskey, and with this fluid at the lofty figure of $125 a gallon, I rarely veer from the even and placid tenor of my ways." A few months later David confided to his family that "the end is near and if we are spared to meet again, I shall thank God it is over."[34]

Yandell's activities during the last year of the war are unclear. He was incapacitated briefly when his hand became badly infected. His colleagues advised amputation, but the surgeon's insistence on delaying the radical procedure saved the hand. In the autumn of 1864 he may have been sent to Tyler, Texas, to combat the "great suffering among the Federal Prisoners" incarcerated there, and there is some evidence that he inspected military hospitals throughout Texas and traveled to Mexico on business for Kirby Smith.[35] However, by the final spring his official duties were insufficient to occupy his time. Illnesses were few, medical supplies were scarce, and military activities had nearly ceased. After the surrender of the Confederate armies east of the Mississippi, the Army of the Trans-Mississippi began to disintegrate. Despite the obvious impending collapse of the Confederacy and Yandell's conviction that the cause was lost, he served his commander to the last. Fearing reprisals from the victorious Federals, Kirby Smith planned to leave the country, and Yandell aided with preparations for the proposed flight; for two months he acted as the general's medical director, adjutant general, and personal secretary combined. When Kirby Smith surrendered on June 1, the doctor was the only staff officer remaining at his post.

Yandell's military career ended June 6 when he and Kirby Smith's chief of secret service arrived in New Orleans and surrendered themselves and $3299 in Confederate funds to General Edward Canby. The doctor was unable to finance his return home. Canby gave him sufficient money for passage to Louisville. [36]

The end of the war found the Yandell family scattered across the South. Fanny and the children were in Louisville, Lunsford and Sally were in West Tennessee, Willie was in Mississippi, and Lunny was stationed in North Carolina. They all had experienced the frightening, dreary, and senseless consequences of war, but they were lucky—they survived unharmed.

For the civilians, anxiety for their loved ones and the privation of necessities were ever present. Fanny and the children experienced hardships in Louisville. Prices were inflated, supplies were scarce, and Fanny lamented that at Christmas there was little more to put in the stockings than "rag dolls hideous enough to scare the little ones . . . Santa Klaus being robbed by the soldiers." [37] Lunsford and Sally also knew depressing times. In November 1861 David had appointed his father to supervise one of the Memphis hospitals, and shortly thereafter Lunsford assumed an additional responsibility when he was ordained to preach in the Memphis Presbytery. When Memphis fell to the Federal forces, Lunsford joined his family at Coral Ridge, his second wife's plantation in West Tennessee, and there he farmed, provided area residents with medical care, and preached at the nearby Dancyville Presbyterian Church. By late summer of 1862 the Yandells were "cut off from the world" and began to suffer the side effects of war.

Federal troops camped on their land, billeted themselves in their house, burned their fences and outhouses, and carried off their stock and food supply. To provide necessities for his family and sixty slaves who depended on him, Lunsford sold several bales of cotton to the Yankees, in violation of Confederate law. During the war he also performed several non-partisan missions of mercy. He worked for the release of two Union surgeons (his former students) held by the Confederates at Columbus, rescued two Confederate sympathizers at Memphis who were under sentence to be executed as spies, and visited a Union prison near Louisville to help a Confederate amputee return to his family near Memphis.[38]

Lunsford and Sally seldom knew the whereabouts or condition of their loved ones, for the wartime mail was erratic and the occasional newspapers, printed on "brown wrapping paper with blurred print," carried frightening rumors as well as depressing news. Unable to purchase dress fabrics for clothes to replace those she outgrew, Sally learned to make new garments from old ones. In her spare time she developed an appreciation for Shakespeare, Milton, Pope, Tennyson, and others whose works filled her father's library, but she pined for the excitement of the gay social life she thought she was missing in Louisville. Lonely, depressed, and worried about the safety of her beloved brothers, the adolescent criticized her father for taking her to the remote area of Tennessee and confided to her diary that she was lonesome enough to "get married to the first good chance I have. Pa cares nothing for me, and I want to run away."[39]

Willie helped his father care for the sick and wounded in the Memphis hospitals, but after the fall of that town he rejoined the army and worked as an assistant surgeon in a Mississippi hospital where he had "plenty of time to read and study medicine in the books and at the bedside."[40] Lunny remained with Hardee's forces throughout the war and was mentioned in many of the general's reports for his "admirable care of the sick and wounded . . . [and] for gallantry on the field of battle." After his surrender at Greensboro, Lunny traveled to Tennessee to visit with his father and Sally, whom he fondly called his "Pet," and then returned to Louisville to practice his profession. In his pocket he carried a reminder of the war—a silver half-dollar presented to him by General Hardee. Impervious to the token's sentimental value, Sally noted that the coin was certainly "little to show for four years of hard work."[41]

David arrived back in Louisville on July 4, 1865, and picked up the remnants of his earlier life as a civilian physician. In the years after the war he kept in touch with several of his former commanders and other army friends and always exhibited pride in having served with the Confederate forces. Claiming that "all of my blood flows in southern veins," he was quick to correct an Englishman who introduced him as a "Yankee doctor," but he seemed unwilling to revel in the glories of the lost cause and urged his colleagues to forget the bitterness that lingered after the war. Nevertheless, he probably smiled at the comments of a friend whose correspondence recalled the pleasant moments during their army days and may have agreed that "as far as we were personally concerned the war was not so bad. It added so much to the number of my friends and acquaintances that had it not been for the villianous [sic] saltpeter, I rather enjoyed it."[42]

The war certainly added to Yandell's list of friends and admirers, but its value to his total career was infinitely greater. During his four years in the army, which he labeled "a great though terrible school," he treated nearly every known medical and surgical problem and increased his professional skills.[43] His administrative responsibilities broadened his understanding of hospital management. The war's most profound effect on Yandell, however, was to sharpen his awareness of the large number of poorly trained and incompetent doctors throughout the nation. To the correction of this inadequacy within his profession, he dedicated the remainder of his life.

4

PROFESSOR OF
SURGERY

WEARY AND PENNILESS, David returned to Louisville in
July 1865, in doubt of being permitted to resume his profession; reprisals against Confederate sympathizers had occurred
in Louisville during the war, and his prominence in the army
medical department was well known. But ten days after his
arrival David opened an office and quickly rebuilt his practice,
for his friends "of both parties met me with more than their
ancient cordiality."[1] He was joined by his father and Lunny,
and for many years the three physicians shared the small office
adjoining the family home on Chestnut Street.

Before the outbreak of the war David and Fanny had con-
templated building a new house, but on their return to Louisville they moved back into the one that had been Lunsford's
residence since 1850. Despite its use by Federal troops during
the early months of the conflict, the Yandell residence had
received minimal damage from the intruders. Lunsford's fine
collection of rare books was missing, but most of the family's
possessions remained unscathed. In 1871 David purchased the
house from his father for $15,000, and he and Fanny lived in
the commodious three-story brick dwelling for the remainder
of their lives. David appreciated the stylish decor of their
home, but his favorite rooms were the library, which he filled

with expensive books, and the dining room, where he displayed hunting tropies collected during his annual expeditions. David hunted from Maine to California and pursued everything from quail to grizzly bear. A large shed in the backyard held the smoked meats from animals he bagged on his outings, and the stable housed his fine hunting dogs as well as his horses.

Large and elegant, the Yandell home could accommodate a variety of visitors. Out-of-town guests, including Generals Hardee and Kirby Smith, enjoyed lengthy visits with the Yandells. Fanny's mother lived with them for many years, and students occasionally boarded with their favorite professor. Moreover, during their first year back in Louisville, Lunsford and his family stayed with David and Fanny until their nearby home was renovated. Apparently the only problem of having two families under one roof centered around Sally's evening activities. David liked to retire early and complained about Sally's going out with her friends, for she awakened him on her "late" (10 o'clock) return. On such occasions David feared that he would be unable to fall asleep again, but Sally noted that he "fumed and fussed himself to sleep in the course of the next five minutes." Except for such occasional conflicts, the Yandells were a congenial clan, and a lazy summer afternoon could find them in a lively discussion or gathered around a basket of homegrown peaches, "racing to see who can eat the fastest and longest." [2]

His immediate family was the pride of David's life. Fanny, a "dutiful, true, brave, honest and wise" wife entertained graciously, but remained in the background while her husband claimed the limelight. [3] A formal and austere woman, who always referred to her husband as "Dr. Yandell," Fanny's activities included membership in a literary society and volunteer work at the city's free kindergarten and at the Children's Hospital (built in 1890), but most of her energies were consumed by caring for her husband and three children.

Susie was the most vivacious of the Yandell children. A "bad tempered little puss" as a child, she exhibited as a young lady a stubborn streak apparently inherited from her father. [4] Her

University of Louisville medical building (left) and academic building, before 1856 fire. From Works Progress Administration, *A Centennial History of the University of Louisville* (Louisville, 1939), p. 60.

Medical Department, University of Louisville, 1876. From *Kentucky State Gazeteer and Business Directory for 1876–1877* (Louisville, 1876), p. 273.

Medical Department, University of Louisville, after 1888. Left wing houses the clinic for which David Yandell campaigned for 20 years. *Courtesy of Kornhauser Health Sciences Library, University of Louisville*

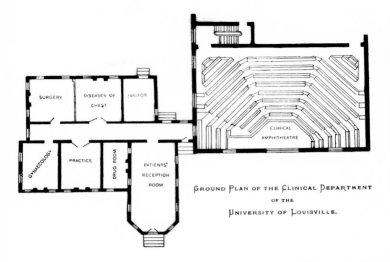

GROUND PLAN OF THE CLINICAL DEPARTMENT
OF THE
UNIVERSITY OF LOUISVILLE.

Ground plan of the clinical department of the University of Louisville
Courtesy of Kornhauser Health Sciences Library
University of Louisville

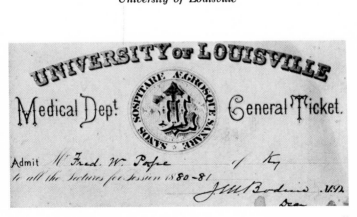

Class ticket for Medical Department of the University of Louisville
Courtesy of John W. Muir, Bardstown, Kentucky

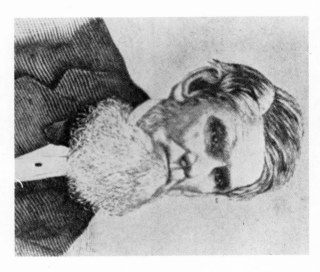

Lunsford Pitts Yandell, Sr.
From J. N. McCormack, *Some of the Medical Pioneers of Kentucky* (Bowling Green, Ky., 1917), p. 90.

David Wendel Yandell, circa 1870
*Courtesy of Kentucky Library
Western Kentucky University*

marriage to James F. Buckner, a Republican and the son of a Louisvillian who served as one of Lincoln's electors in 1864, caused quite a commotion in the Yandell home. David could forgive his daughter for choosing a man whose family connections had been pro-Union, for many of his friends had opposed the Confederacy. But he refused to accept a Republican into his household, and for several years father and daughter were estranged. Neither would apologize for the heated words that passed between them before the wedding.

Maria inherited the more docile, sweet nature of her mother. She was an accomplished pianist but her talents were exhibited only for family and close friends. In 1872 she married Dr. William O. Roberts, one of Yandell's former students and medical assistants. The young doctor, who lived with them during his student days, not only won the affections of their daughter, he perhaps replaced the son the Yandells lost several years earlier.

The tragedy occurred in August 1866, when the Yandell children were visiting with Fanny's sister and brother-in-law, Elizabeth and General George Maney, and had gone to the Cumberland River to find relief from the oppressive heat. Wading out too far, the eleven-year-old Allison and his cousin were caught up by the swift current and swept away from the other children. A seventeen-year-old boy heard their cries for help and rescued the general's son, but in his efforts to save Allison, they both drowned. Allison's body, recovered the following day, was taken to Louisville by his grieving parents for burial. Several of David's friends later remarked that the doctor's great compassion for children, especially young boys, probably stemmed from the loss of his own son. The doctor was a favorite with Louisville children, who found him a soft touch for a buggy ride or a handout of candy and pennies.

The small medical office that adjoined his home was the scene of much activity, since David, Lunny, and their father kept regular office hours each day. Many of their patients were charity cases or paid their bills with commodities; as a young boy Abraham Flexner took freshly baked bread to Lunny to pay for his father's extended medical care.[5] Despite the large percentage of nonpaying patients, the Yandells' collection of fees eventually provided relatively comfortable livings for their families. When Lunsford returned to Louisville in 1867, his finances were in such precarious shape that he was forced to sell some of his wife's Tennessee property to pay for remodeling and redecorating his home, and he asked David to request that Willie's tuition at the medical school be waived. However, by the early 1870s his annual collections averaged $3,000, then a handsome sum. Lunny made enough money during his first two years of postwar practice to finance his long-awaited study in Europe. Shortly after his marriage to Louise Elliston of Nashville, he and his bride spent a year in France and Germany. While Lunny worked in the hospitals under the European masters, Louise studied art.

No records of David's finances have been found, but his fees probably were the standard ones of the era—three dollars for housecalls, two dollars for office visits, thirty dollars for routine obstetrical cases—and his collections probably were equal to those of his father and brother. Many of David's patients were wealthy political and social figures from Louisville and nearby communities. One of his wealthiest, and most eccentric, patients was Sally Ward, Louisville's glamorous belle. A rebel against conventional behavior, Sally refused to enter David's office and mingle with the "common people." When she wanted medications she had her carriage pulled up in front of David's house, and he prescribed for her in its elegant interior rather than in his office.

For several years David also conducted a medical practice in the old section of town. Adhering to the admonitions of Daniel Drake to "lend a willing ear to the calls of the poor," David established another free outpatient dispensary, the Louisville Clinic, for the city's indigents. There, he and an old army friend provided medical care for the city's poor and gave supervised training to a few private students. David's protégés were impressed with his charitable works at the clinic and in his private practice. He frequently paid the bills of destitute patients he referred to the city's hospitals, and others, whose finicky or alcoholic appetites might prohibit them from obtaining proper nourishment, he took home to dine at his laden table. On at least one occasion he slipped money to an unfortunate, claiming, "By G——, no one can say he ever left my office empty handed."[6] Yandell provided round-the-clock care for acutely ill patients and was known to supply destitute families with groceries, under the tactful guise that the patient needed special foods. Many of his shut-in patients received special treats in the summertime; David was frequently seen driving a blossom-filled buggy, delivering bouquets from his garden to his patients as he made the daily round of house-calls.

A sizable portion of David's and Lunny's income was derived from their teaching at the university. Ticket fees varied from $10 to $15 per instructor during the postwar era. Enrollment records are unavailable, but the student body usually numbered slightly more than twice the number of graduates, which ranged from 47 in 1868 to 104 in 1892. Remuneration for the few hours involved during the brief annual session could be handsome. Lunsford was asked to rejoin the faculty after his return to Louisville, but he refused. His failure to salvage the Memphis Medical College and his general disgust with faculty feuding dampened his interest in teaching. He devoted the remainder of his life to practicing medicine, writing medical treatises, and preaching at the Presbyterian church on Walnut Street. Nevertheless, the senior Yandell remained concerned about the university and its progress and undoubtedly was a source of encouragement and inspiration to his sons who served on the faculty. His death in 1878 was mourned not only by his family but also by hundreds of his former students and fellow practitioners, whose professional lives had been enriched by Lunsford's efforts to advance medical knowledge.

In 1867 David rejoined the university as professor of clinical medicine and two years later became professor of clinical surgery. The school had made few changes in the two decades since his student days. The physical plant and curriculum were about the same, although the faculty had changed (and with few exceptions was composed of men less able than those to whom David had listened). The school still had a four-month year, ungraded courses, and no laboratory facilities or classes, except for dissection. Students were taught by lecture, recitation, and demonstration, and the city hospital amphitheater eight blocks away provided the school's only clinical facilities, which students were urged but not required to visit. Frequent quizzes had replaced the writing of a thesis; yet grades were not kept. The oral examination continued as a graduation requirement, but few students ever failed to receive a degree. Occasionally even the examination was disregarded. A postwar student told of one of his oral examinations, probably conducted by Yandell.

"Pull up your chair," said the examiner. "I want every shot to count."

"Fire away, Professor," responded the student. "I have been in worse quarters than this."

"What do you mean?" asked the Professor.

"I was at the Battle of Shiloh and saw you on the battlefield. You were on General Johnson's [*sic*] staff and looked well on horseback."

Remarking that anyone who survived Shiloh was "capable of practicing medicine in Kentucky," the teacher canceled the questioning period and invited the student to dine with him.[7]

Many of the professors held their students in fond regard, but local citizens viewed them as a rowdy, uncouth element to be shunned by polite society, for they emitted the characteristic odor of decayed laboratory specimens, and many of them carried guns and knives and were notorious for not paying their debts. On numerous occasions the faculty interceded in the behalf of students arrested for gambling, drinking, fighting, burglary, and grave robbing. That last offense probably gave the faculty their greatest disciplinary problem, for although they could not appear to condone such activities, they were aware of the difficulty in acquiring subjects legally.

The school itself had to practice a great deal of ingenuity to obtain cadavers. Unclaimed bodies at the city morgue were sent to the university, and occasionally a corpse was "rented" from its impoverished heirs and returned to them for burial when the students had completed their study of it. But when legal means produced insufficient specimens, more daring measures were required. In 1863 the school's dean, J. W. Benson, was arrested on suspicion of stealing bodies from the Freedmen's Bureau hospital. During the early years of his career, Yandell obtained his own cadavers, but in the latter part of the century this macabre work was performed for the departments of anatomy and surgery by a professional. Upon receiving information of the death and impending burial of an inmate of the workhouse, prison, or local charity hospital, Yandell hired a "quiet, discreet [and] prudent" professional "resurrectionist," usually the school janitor, to procure the body. Although state law explicitly forbade body snatching, few complaints were made unless bodies were exhumed from private cemeteries. Occasionally mishaps occurred. One resurrectionist, believing someone had fired shots at him, fled and left the object of his night's work in the doctor's buggy. The next morning Yandell discovered that his faithful steed had ambled back home with the incriminating but apparently yet undetected corpse sprawled across the vehicle's front seat.[8]

Student involvement in grave robbing, despite school policy against it, was reported in the Louisville press throughout the postwar period and editorials pleaded for a change in the state's laws. An 1890 article in the *Courier-Journal* quoted Yandell at length about the need for dissection subjects and the means by which medical schools were forced to obtain them. Yandell estimated that between 1837 and 1890 more than 4,000 cadavers had been used by the university and the town's other medical schools; most of them were secured by unorthodox means.

They may have been law-breaking rowdies outside of class, but most students exhibited the manners and deportment of gentlemen in Professor Yandell's presence. The Yandell home was the frequent site of late-evening discussions between students and teacher concerning medicine, hunting, and almost any subject except politics. Students who were short of funds knew they were welcome at the professor's table, where the family cook's mouth-watering dishes and a fine selection of wines were served in abundance.

Despite his tenderness towards his students, Yandell was better remembered by them for his oratorical and surgical skills. Each annual session commenced and ended with a special lecture, and during the three decades he was an active member of the faculty, Yandell delivered many of these addresses. His selection of topics covered a wide variety of medically related fields, and all were filled with subtle wit and advice and exhibited his skill in weaving together history, literature, and medicine. One of his most interesting introductory orations was the discourse in memory of an associate, Lewis Rogers. Exhibiting few of the overblown superlatives characteristic of biographical works of the era, David's address was a sensitive salute to his friend and inspirational challenge to his listeners. Rogers had been one of Louisville's leading doctors and a member of the university's faculty. Praising Rogers' careful training and disciplined mind, Yandell labeled his friend "the most practical of all the scientific teachers and the most scientific of all the practical teachers of medicine I have ever known." Although he used Rogers as an example for students to emulate, Yandell lamented that his learned colleague shared so little of his knowledge with others. Had he taken notes on his cases, Yandell pointed out, he could have "written with profit to the profession as well as his own reputation."[9] The advisability of note-taking in the classroom and later in private practice was one of Yandell's major themes. To encourage the former and thus establish a good habit that might lead to the latter, Yandell annually presented a gold medal to the graduate who had taken the best notes in his surgery classes.

In another of his introductory lectures Yandell acquainted the students with two things on which he placed great emphasis—progress and practicality. Answering those who pointed to some remote past as the golden age in medicine and at the same time chiding colleagues who complacently contented themselves with the "dazzling achievements of the present," he stressed that "there is constant improvement because there is constant discontentment. If there were perfect satisfaction with the present, we should cease to contrive, to labor and save." Many professors expounded theories; David was interested in the practical.

He is the successful teacher who enriches the minds of his pupils with the greatest number of valuable facts—who, at the same time that he makes them learned about disease, makes them also handy in its treatment, who brings before them human ailments in the greatest variety of form, and instructs them how they may be relieved. . . . It will be our constant endeavor to render our courses of instruction useful to you—to illustrate everything that can be made more plain or impressive by models or apparatus, or morbid preparations, or the living subjects of disease. We are nothing if not practical.[10]

Practical. That was the key to Yandell's approach to medical education.

Yandell had "few equals and no superiors" as a teacher and surgeon, and his well-organized lectures were flavored with bits of medical history and witty advice that made his classes interesting and easy to follow.[11] Before and after each demonstration Yandell discussed the various theories and treatments of the malady through the ages and usually qualified his opinion of the most effective care with remarks about the probability that better medications and techniques would be devised in the future. His students were urged to keep abreast of, and be open minded to, new ideas but to use discretion in adopting them, for "if one half of all the 'certain cures' were but certain, the practice of medicine would be too simple to demand special study or require trained followers."[12]

The desirability of knowing when to act with haste and when to proceed with deliberate caution was another of his frequent admonitions. Many problems, if left to nature, would cure themselves, Yandell advised. Nevertheless, a physician should never neglect the pleas of his patients. Yandell delighted in telling a story about George IV, whose regular physician was too busy to attend to his request for immediate care of a small tumor on the royal derrière. Another doctor was called, the tumor removed, and the new doctor was made a baronet by his grateful sovereign—an excessive reward for the rendered service. But, beamed Yandell, the story served to warn all doctors that "it is not always safe to postpone until the afternoon attending to messages left for you in the morning."[13]

In all treatments he advised persistence in aiding the infirm and the use of conservative measures before resorting to more extreme ones. Yandell's success in avoiding radical procedures was well demonstrated to his students in 1874 through his care of Jeremiah Sullivan Black, a prominent Pennsylvania lawyer who was a former United States attorney general and secretary of state during the Buchanan administration. A passenger on the Louisville and Nashville Railroad en route through Louisville, Black had his arm "shattered" from wrist to shoulder in a freak accident. Because of the high incidence of infection and indeed death from multiple and compound fractures, amputation was the standard treatment in such cases. The doctors at Saint Joseph's Hospital advised that Black's arm be removed immediately, but the patient requested that Dr. Yandell be called for consultation. Yandell studied the injured arm and concluded that a plaster cast, which would mask early signs of infection, could not be used but that manual traction might succeed. He set the bones in their proper places and secured several teams of medical students to hold the bones together day and night until a complete union was effected. Black reportedly regained full use of his arm, the students learned a valuable lesson in medical techniques, and, according to editor Henry Watterson, the grateful L & N paid Yandell a handsome fee for saving the arm and thus preventing a lawsuit against the company.

The preservation of human dignity was another of Yandell's concerns, and throughout his lectures and demonstrations he continually reminded his students that all patients, whatever their wretched state, were entitled to the same respect and care as that given to the wealthiest and most influential person. One of his former students recalled that during a classroom examination of a syphilitic patient from the city hospital, several students began to snicker. Rising to his full height, Yandell remanded the disturbers to silence with a withering look while the patient was removed from the room. After several moments of deafening quiet, Yandell scolded:

If I were old and poor and sick and wretched and had come to this clinic for relief and had heard that hollow, heartless laugh, I would think less kindly of doctors than I had thought before. Nobody comes to the public hospital but the poor, the friendless and the wretched. This unhappy man, the victim of his own sin, has come here to die. What is it to be prostrated by such a disease? It is suffering upon suffering, and death. I would not have that loathsome disease for all the influence and power of the kings and potentates of the old world; for all the shining wealth that ever passed through the golden gates of the peaceful ocean.[14]

Yandell's talent that most impressed his students was his dexterity with a scalpel. Minor procedures were performed on hospital inmates or dispensary patients, but the more difficult and unusual operations were done on cadavers. As he explained his every move, Yandell "cut to the line and to the required depth with geometric precision" and he found his way through "a labyrinthine of surgical spaces with a certainty and safety to the patient which savored of magic."[15] Unfortunately, many of the students in attendance were unable to see the intricate work of their instructor's knife, for they were ten to thirty feet away, and their view was impaired by a variety of obstacles. Yandell's articulate and detailed explanations helped compensate for this, and if the students' knowledge of anatomy was sufficient, they mentally visualized what they were unable to see. Occasionally, advanced students were permitted to help with the demonstrations, but the limited time and space prevented most of them from gaining any real practical experience in surgery, an educational shortcoming that Yandell abhorred.

Yandell's dressings were "beautiful" and his treatment of incisions and wounds was characterized by a scrupulous cleanliness which, prior to the triumphs of antiseptic surgery, was unusual. But despite his skill with the scalpel and his insistence on cleanliness, the art as practiced by the physician was crude and septic by modern standards.

Yandell's operating attire was a freshly laundered coat, but most surgeons and their assistants wore old coats and aprons to protect street clothing. Elsewhere, even these cautions were considered unnecessary. During examinations in the office, home, hospital ward, or lying-in chamber the need for removal of a doctor's jacket to prevent its soiling was obviated by rolling up the sleeves. A gentleman never appeared with his coat off, especially in the presence of a lady.

Yandell scrubbed his hands with green soap, the strongest known cleansing agent, before attending to his patients and insisted that the same preparation be used on his instruments, despite the prevailing belief that anything more than wiping them with a soft damp cloth would dull their cutting edge. During the last fifteen years of the century, instruments were cleaned with a 5-percent solution of carbolic acid; sterilization by heat was not used until the twentieth century.

Throughout most of his career Yandell treated all incisions with compounds of iodine, bromine, and carbolic acid, for he believed that these lessened the chance of severe infection and aided in the cure of suppurating wounds. In the use of these germ-killing agents, he was ahead of his time. But other practices of the day negated many of the benefits derived from the antiseptic agents. Masks, gowns, and gloves were not worn, and patients were not scrubbed or draped before surgery. Hands and instruments were rinsed occasionally during operations with nonsterile water to remove dried blood and other sticky matter. Waxed silk, the most popular suturing material, traditionally was strung through the surgeon's lapel buttonhole for quick and easy access. Each physician made his own bandages from strips of coarsely woven cloth. Boiled to remove the sizing, the strips were then saturated with various medicines, hung to dry, and rolled and stored in glass containers. Surgical sponges were washed in limewater and reused.

Many of the simplest diagnostic aids were unavailable to Yandell and his colleagues, and considering the primitive means with which they determined the nature and extent of disease, the degree of their success is amazing. The thermometer and stethoscope were introduced about midcentury, and David was among the first doctors in Louisville to use them regularly. Blood counts, urinalyses, x-ray studies, and blood pressure readings were unknown until the turn of the century; histology, bacteriology, and microbiology were specialties of the future. Medical histories of patients, when kept at all, were meager, and few doctors or hospitals recorded and systematically filed them for future reference.

By modern standards medical education at the University of Louisville and elsewhere was extremely inadequate. Most medical students entered the school with little academic background and left it with virtually no experience in treating patients. Many of them probably felt as ill prepared as did an 1869 graduate who could "never forget the sinking feeling that came over me when I unfolded this sacred document [his diploma] in the privacy of my own room and realized how little I knew and how incompetent I was to undertake the care of those in the distress of sickness or accident."[16] Understanding this feeling of incompetence, Yandell urged his students to take advantage of postgraduate studies at schools in the East and in Europe.

Although their schooling lacked many of the important aspects of modern medical education, Yandell's students learned basic essentials that aided their professional growth in the rapidly expanding field. Several of the distinguished physicians and surgeons of the late nineteenth and early twentieth centuries received their early training with Yandell—Drs. Lewis Frank and William O. Roberts, professors of surgery at the University of Louisville; Dr. James M. Matthews, father of modern proctology; Dr. John A. Wyeth, founder of the nation's first postgraduate medical school (New York Polyclinic Hospital and Medical School), who was also an AMA president and the originator of a variety of surgical procedures; Dr. Ap Morgan Vance, Kentucky's first orthopedic surgeon, who developed several techniques for correcting bone deformities; Dr.

William L. Rodman, professor of surgery at the Medical College of Philadelphia, who developed a widely acclaimed surgical procedure used in cases of breast cancer; and Dr. Simon Flexner, pathologist, bacteriologist, and director of the Rockefeller Institute of Medical Research.

During Yandell's lengthy postwar association with the University of Louisville, conflicts constantly enveloped the faculty. Fragile, easily bruised egos were ever present; financial problems were all-encompassing. In the resulting faculty feuds the main purpose of their association frequently seemed secondary to the individual's prerogative. Each professor guarded his own sphere of expertise so zealously that the bylaws carried the suggestion that a teacher "in his lectures shall touch as little as possible on the branches of his colleagues."[17] Turnover in the faculty, especially during the decade following the war, was frequent as disgruntled members resigned. Many of them formed new schools in Louisville or joined existing medical institutions in the Midwest that competed with the university for students and their fees. This rivalry impeded rather than stimulated the university's progress.

The creation of the Kentucky School of Medicine in 1850 had provided the university with its first major competition, and the decline in the number of students attending the university was hastened by the Civil War. Before the school recuperated from the drastically reduced enrollment, the Louisville Medical College was established in 1869 with the Hospital College of Medicine chartered five years later. In addition the 1874 state legislature passed a law that required all new physicians to be graduates of medical schools. The act was designed to eliminate quacks and charlatans who posed as qualified doctors, but since it stipulated neither guidelines nor minimum standards for medical schools, the law only encouraged the growth of diploma mills. Many of these sprang up to provide a quick and cheap route to a degree devoid of any educational merit. The creation of medical schools in adjoining states paralleled that in Kentucky, and with all these schools the university had to compete.

The faculty of the University of Louisville attempted to solve the financial bind in a variety of ways. On several occasions vacated chairs were not immediately filled, and the teachers doubled up on their duties so that tuition could be reduced by the price of a single ticket. An unsuccessful attempt was also made to derive additional income for the endowment of several chairs by leasing out most of the university's land. Summer school sessions were taught, especially when competing schools offered them, in the hope of attracting a few additional students, and efforts were made to get all midwestern schools to standardize their fees and curriculum. None of these measures was successful. All attempts to upgrade requirements and facilities were hampered by the competing schools. Ease in obtaining a diploma attracted more students than did educational opportunities; a school with rigid entrance and graduation requirements or expanded facilities that would raise the tuition was a school with too few students to survive.

Yandell was interested in all the problems faced by the school and fought for measures that would improve the educational opportunities it could offer. But the improvement for which he fought the hardest was the expansion of facilities. The best medical education, Yandell believed, was a practical one that included a wide variety of clinical opportunities, for clinical teaching was the "alpha and omega" of a good education. "By studying medicine in the laboratory, under the microscope, at the dissecting-table, in the wards of the hospitals and in the dispensaries where patients are seen, examined, and prescribed for, and where, by attending to what are now so often called the refinements of chemistry and physics, students learn the diagnosis of disease as well as its treatment."[18] Providing opportunities for the bedside study of disease was his major concern, and attempting to solve problems involved in improving the school's clinical facilities dominated Yandell's career.

The outpatient Stokes Dispensary Yandell founded before the war was operated briefly by several of his university associates after he joined the Confederate army, but in 1864 the university built its own dispensary, a small, one-story brick building located about thirty feet to the rear of the medical school. The faculty assumed most of the construction costs and outfitted the structure with all necessary paraphernalia. Drs. Thomas Satterwhite and John Goodman, who paid a small portion of the building expenses, were contracted to manage the facility and to supply the university's clinical lectures with patients whose maladies would be of interest for classroom demonstrations. To compensate for their services the managers were given the right to use the facility to treat private patients and to teach private students, and the school encouraged its students to enroll for the instructions, which carried a fee of $50 per year. During the summer when the medical school was not in session private lessons were conducted by a dispensary corporation consisting of both faculty and nonfaculty instructors. Thus the dispensary provided demonstration subjects for the school and incomes for those who used its free teaching advantages. The average student derived little direct benefit from it.

There is a dearth of information about either the university dispensary or those founded by Yandell, but the 1868 *Louisville Municipal Report* gives a grim description of the Eastern and Western dispensaries, clinics operated by the city for the "worthy subjects of medical charity" who "preferred to suffer in silence rather than to submit to examination . . . in the presence of medical students."[19] The city clinics were smaller than those operated by Yandell and the school, and they treated only 1,500 of the town's 6,000 clinic cases, but all four facilities probably were similar in their operation.

Located in large rooms previously used for storage, the city's clinics were partitioned into four compartments. The reception area was outfitted with wooden benches to accommodate waiting patients. The consultation room, where the volunteer doctor examined, diagnosed, and prescribed, contained a table, stove, chair, and bench. Next to the drug room,

74

where medicines were dispensed, was a small area equipped with a bed and washstand for the resident apothecary. Included among the medical paraphernalia were forceps, glass syringes, probes, sounds, specula, one hypodermic syringe, one catheter, one ophthalmoscope, one small pocket case of instruments, and fourteen yards of flannel for bandages. Nearly every imaginable malady was treated, but the major complaints were respiratory and intestinal disorders, venereal diseases, and intermittent, remittent, and continued fevers. Patients requiring surgery were sent to the hospitals.

When Yandell had opened his large and efficiently organized Louisville Clinic in 1866, it attracted many students and gave the university's dispensary noticeable competition. A few months after he rejoined the faculty in the late spring of 1867, Drs. Satterwhite and Goodman complained loudly to the faculty because David was allowed to continue his clinic; they believed that his position as a professor gave his dispensary an "immense advantage" over the university's facility. Yandell offered to "divide the influence of his name and services equally between the two Dispensaries, to lecture an equal number of times to each and receive no fee from either," but his offer was refused. When the faculty passed a resolution that prohibited professors from conducting private classes that competed with those offered by the school, Yandell complained bitterly about the faculty's ex post facto ruling. He refused to sever his connection with the Louisville Clinic, for to do so would "be to the injury of public teaching in Louisville and unfriendly to the interests of the Med. Dept. of the University."[20] Faculty pressure, however, forced him to rescind his decision.

A few weeks after Yandell's retirement from the Louisville Clinic, he began a crusade to enlarge the university's own dispensary, which he complained was not spacious enough to accommodate the school's students either in small groups or for class instruction. Yandell also suggested that a clinical amphitheater be erected adjoining the dispensary, for many students were unable to attend the demonstrations at the city hospital because of inclement weather during the wintery school term. A committee was appointed to confer with Drs. Satterwhite and Goodman, and a suggestion to redesign one of the lecture rooms as an amphitheater and to connect it to the existing dispensary was substituted for Yandell's idea. This plan was presented to the faculty, but nothing was gained by the effort; the faculty was still in debt for the construction of the original clinic and refused to increase its financial burden.

Undaunted, Yandell and several colleagues devised a plan to obtain an income so that fees could be reduced, several chairs endowed, and improved clinical facilities made available. Much of the University Square was unused; if it were portioned into twenty-four small building lots it could be leased for at least $3,000 annually. Yandell and two other faculty members presented a petition to this effect to the university's Board of Trustees, who regretted that they did not possess the power to approve the scheme. Only the mayor and his council could consent to such an undertaking, and they refused to do so.

The faculty then tendered a resolution that the mayor and council allow the medical school to use the university's academic building (at the time occupied rent-free by Male High School) as a hospital to be maintained at the expense of the city and governed by the mayor and his council. The university president and Board of Trustees would reserve the right to appoint physicians and surgeons to attend its inmates, and the patients, who would receive free care from the faculty, could be studied by the students. The scheme would have established one of the first modern teaching hospitals in the nation, but the mayor and his council declined to consider the idea.

The defeat of Yandell's plan to expand the clinical facilities coincided with a major faculty feud concerning appointments and titles—a conflict that was typical of medical schools of the era. During the feud Yandell resigned from the school, disgusted with his fellow faculty members, who were equally disgruntled with his overbearing attempts to accomplish his pet project. Two other professors who sympathized with his efforts also resigned. A few weeks later Lunny joined the faculty.

The war had matured Lunny, and his studies in Europe had increased his knowledge and self-confidence. Several years earlier he surmised that if he could acquire "Willie's [mild] temper, brother David's beautiful manners, Pa's talent for writing and talking and brother David's skill as a physician, I should be a remarkable and remarkably satisfied man."[21] Apparently, Lunny possessed a sizable portion of each of these attributes, for during his university career he became widely known for his lectures and writings on dermatology and his editorial efforts for a weekly medical magazine, the *Louisville Medical News*. After he joined the faculty, Lunny began to act as a peacemaker between his new colleagues and David and a year later succeeded in ending their quarrel. The two brothers worked together for improvements. Lunny was more politic than David and slower to anger, but together they hammered away at the complacent faculty, urging and demanding reforms that would upgrade the education received by the university's students. Their favorite crusade was the enlarged dispensary.

When David returned to the faculty in June 1869, he promised that he would give the school his "best endeavors to advance its usefullness and prosperity" and would make a cordial effort "to secure that harmony [among the faculty] which I feel essential to success."[22] His colleagues, who expressed some reservations in inviting the tempest to rejoin them, interpreted his promise as a pledge to desist in the campaign to force them into greater financial difficulties. They were quite mistaken. For two years he made no official mention of the project, but in the summer of 1871 Yandell armed himself with drawings and building estimates and recommenced his badgering. Again, the faculty turned down the plan. They had due a $4,000 bill for paving the streets adjoining the school's property and felt that in view of this expense, the proposed project would involve them more than would be "expedient or profitable."[23]

For the remainder of the 1870s the subject of enlarging the dispensary was discussed in private but not in faculty meetings. During this interim Yandell embarked on another scheme. In conversing with the wealthy Louisvillian Shakespeare Caldwell, Yandell remarked that most of the nation's hospitals, including the two in Louisville, were filled with incurables; little space was available for convalescents. Were he ever to manage a hospital, said the physician. he would "admit only cases of acute and otherwise curable diseases."[24] Caldwell wished to erect an appropriate memorial to his recently departed wife, and Yandell sensed the possibility of building a hospital that would supply even greater advantages for students than he had hoped for with the enlarged clinic. Saints Mary and Elizabeth Hospital resulted from Caldwell's benevolence and was opened for use in June 1874.

When plans for the four-story hospital were announced, the school offered part of University Square for it to be built upon, but a site at Thirteenth and Magnolia was chosen instead. Had it been built adjoining the medical school it could have been the teaching hospital of which Yandell dreamed. Nevertheless, the doctor convinced Caldwell to allow the university's faculty to furnish medical and surgical services for impoverished patients and to use the new facility as a teaching hospital where students could gain bedside experience and aid in treating patients. Within a few years this scheme proved unsuccessful, for some of the professors were unwilling to devote sufficient time to instructing and supervising students outside of their scheduled classroom duties, and the distance between the school and the hospital discouraged many students from taking advantage of it.

The failure of the Saints Mary and Elizabeth Hospital to double as a teaching hospital for the university dampened Yandell's spirits, but only temporarily. In 1882, shortly after a $477 legacy was received by the school for the improvement of its clinic, Yandell recommenced his nagging. He suggested that if each professor added to the gift by contributing a small portion of his ticket money, the project could be financed. The suggestion was met with overwhelming disapproval. Two years later he again raised the question of the dispensary, and when the faculty gave their usual answer, Yandell again submitted his resignation. Throughout most of his seventeen-year battle for the facility, he had been backed by his brother, but Lunny's death in March of 1884 had robbed him of his most faithful and constant supporter. In his letter of resignation Yandell delivered a blistering attack against his colleagues, whom he accused of being disinterested in the quality of education they provided. The "clinical facilities of the university are much behind what they should be and could be," Yandell scolded. Fearing the loss of the school's most noted professor, the faculty promised that if he rescinded his resignation, they would consider the dispensary question the following year. Yandell honored their request but warned that he would expect results soon, for the dispensary was "very near to his heart."[25]

The following year Yandell asked the Board of Trustees to inspect the school's physical plant and determine what they could do to assist the faculty in "advancing their interests of attaching a hospital or enlarged dispensary" to its facilities.[26] A year later the drawings for a new dispensary were submitted by H. P. McDonald Brothers, a construction company, and the board agreed to contract the work. The university's treasurer converted into cash some city bonds that the school had held for years, and a loan was secured by the faculty and the board to finance the remainder of the building. The dispensary was completed in the early months of 1888.

The new dispensary was attached to one of the large lecture rooms, which was remodeled into an amphitheater. The structure contained a 20-by-36-foot waiting room and four smaller examination and treatment rooms for the departments of surgery, gynecology, medicine, and thoracic diseases. A room for drug storage and another for the janitor's use completed the building. After twenty years of crusading, Yandell finally had his dispensary where groups of students could receive practical diagnostic and therapeutic training by treating patients under the supervision of their instructors.

Another of Yandell's crusades that took nearly twenty years

to accomplish was the creation of internships in Louisville's various hospitals. Believing that students needed more practical experience than they could obtain during their brief stay at the university, he tried to institute the French system of postgraduate work. Provisions for the plan had been written into the school's bylaws before the war, but the program had not been implemented. Later, when Yandell tried to introduce the internship program, he ran into a variety of frustrating problems. The city's hospitals wanted the positions made available to graduates of all the medical schools, but the schools could never agree on how the recipients should be selected or who should supervise the program. After years of haggling, the Kentucky School of Medicine and the university agreed to select interns from their 1885 spring graduates to work for a year in the hospitals. Selection of the interns was based on academic merit. Unfortunately, there were only a half-dozen positions—and several hundred graduates eager to benefit from the program.

Other appointments provided learning and teaching experience for young graduates. By the last decade of the century every professor was aided by a demonstrator or assistant whose salary he paid from his own pocket and whose work he was supposed to supervise closely. The curriculum also was expanded and the faculty was enlarged. By 1900 four six-month sessions were required for a degree. For all of these improvements Yandell had worked, though not as vigorously as he toiled to enlarge the dispensary.

Yandell's interest in education also extended to the city's public schools, and in the postwar decade he was elected to serve two terms on the Louisville School Board. During his four years on the board, he worked on several committees and headed its sanitary affairs group. Here, too, Yandell's suggestions were met with an unfortunate lack of money, for although he brought to the board's attention some of the abominable health and safety conditions that existed in the schools, the funds to correct them were not available. Always supportive of suggestions to increase salaries, expand facilities, and broaden the curriculum, Yandell was a staunch opponent of severe punishment of pupils. On several occasions the doctor introduced resolutions that chastised teachers for their harsh disciplinary measures and suggested that "a repetition of the conduct will be deemed an offense inviting dismissal."[27]

Yandell's career was characterized by campaigns for educational improvements, but feuds that involved his ego erupted occasionally and influenced his judgment. His colleagues at the university apparently valued his association with the school enough to give in to most of Yandell's demands. Although he favored the creation of additional chairs and assistantships, the threat of a younger man in his own domain provoked an uproar that illustrates how zealously he guarded against any infringement upon his status.

The trouble started in 1871, when George Bayless, professor of principles and practice of surgery, requested that his load at the school be lightened because of his advanced age and ill health. Richard Cowling was appointed as Bayless's adjunct professor. Yandell thundered a protest. Students desired lectures given by professors, not assistants, Yandell warned, and to divide the surgical instruction between three men (Yandell was professor of clinical surgery) would endanger the good of the school, for "each would leave work for others to do with the results—neglect of important topics." Yandell's objections were ignored. Two years later Bayless died and Cowling, his obvious successor, was suggested to fill the senior surgeon's chair. Again Yandell objected and demanded that the surgical position be renamed, for to give to Cowling the title previously held by Bayless, the senior member of the surgical department, would injure Yandell's name "in the eyes of the public, as by doing so the faculty would place a junior over the head of a senior." He was "Cowling's superior in age both as a man and as a teacher," Yandell proclaimed. Anxious for harmony, the faculty agreed to Yandell's demands.[28]

Following Cowling's death in 1881 Yandell briefly assumed the responsibilities of the entire surgical department, but he soon discovered that his health would not permit the extra burden. Lunny suggested to the faculty that W. O. Roberts, David's son-in-law, replace Cowling. Several members of the faculty opposed the appointment lest the school "lay itself open to the charge of nepotism," a practice that was nearly as commonplace in medical schools as it was in politics. Yandell's threatened wrath convinced them of the advisability of the appointment, and the well-qualified Roberts was named professor of surgical pathology and operative surgery.[29] During the late 1880s and early 1890s he performed many of the surgical demonstrations for his father-in-law, whose dexterity with a scalpel was hampered occasionally by bouts of rheumatism.

Gruff, egotistical, even arrogant in his relations with his professional associates, Yandell was famous among his friends for his charm and wit. Henry Watterson, editor of the *Courier-Journal* and a powerful force in state politics, enjoyed bird hunting with Yandell, and the two men attended many local functions together. Watterson recorded an anecdote about a vaudeville show they visited. The impresario of one of the acts issued a challenge to all onlookers to beat his poker-playing pig, and Yandell suggested they accept the challenge. "We sat at the table with the hog, on the stage, and did our best. The hog beat us. He did not handle the cards, but he indicated the cards to be played. I could not understand, nor could Dave."[30]

Reuben Durrett was another of Yandell's close friends. Both men enjoyed discussing history, and they and other members of The Filson Club, a private society founded by Durrett in 1884 and dedicated to the collection and publication of historic matter, gathered in Durrett's library to discuss events of the commonwealth's past. Frequent visitors to the Yandell home included Durrett; Douglas Sherley, a wealthy bachelor for whom Yandell's daughters frequently served as hostesses; Milton H. Smith, president of the L & N Railroad; old confederates Basil Duke, William Preston, and John B. Castleman; and Governor J. Proctor Knott, who appointed Yandell surgeon general of the Kentucky militia. Many of the physician's friends were fellow members of the Pendennis Club (a private men's club), the Salmagundi Club (a social and literary club for men), and the Louisville Kennel Club, which Yandell founded in 1894.

Another welcome visitor to the Yandell home was Lunny's talented daughter Enid. Endowed with her mother's artistic abilities, Enid graduated from The Cincinnati Academy of Art and studied sculpture in Paris with Rodin. Among her best-known works is the large statue of Daniel Boone in Louisville's Cherokee Park. Following Lunny's death in 1884 David assumed some of the parental and financial responsibilities for Enid and was extremely proud of her talent. But when he learned that she accepted payment for her sculpture, he was horrified and declared that her independence was a "family disgrace," for she was "the first woman of the name who ever earned a dollar for herself."[31] Not everyone shared her uncle's abhorrence of Enid's career; during her lifetime she won many honors in the United States and in Europe and is remembered as one of the nation's finest sculptors.

During the 1870s and early 1880s a variety of distinguished guests visited Louisville, and David Yandell was among the city's hosts who entertained them. He aided in the preparations for the 1872 visit of the Grand Duke Alexis, third son of the Czar of Russia, and for the brief sojourn of Emperor Dom Pedro II of Brazil four years later. The Brazilian ruler was more interested in visiting Kentucky's caves than in socializing, but the Russian enjoyed a grand ball and banquet held in his honor. Among the ladies presented to the duke were Fanny Yandell and her teenage daughters. The duke, a true politician, informed a newspaper reporter that Louisville could boast some of the most beautiful women he saw during his visit to the United States.

Yandell's fondness for playing host to visiting dignitaries overpowered his dislike for Republicans, and he helped entertain three Republican presidents. In 1877 twelve Kentuckians, including Yandell, escorted President Rutherford B. Hayes from Cincinnati to the Falls City. As the doctor and the future supreme court justice John Marshall Harlan were engaged in conversation on the platform of the presidential railroad car, the physician was mistaken for the president by a young bootblack and was offered a free shine. The tale of the mistaken identity was heartily enjoyed by the entire party. When former president Ulysses S. Grant visited Louisville two years later, Yandell again was part of the greeting committee, and at a luncheon honoring Grant, Yandell sat at the head table and entertained the old general with stories of his own Civil War escapades.

President Chester A. Arthur journeyed to Louisville in 1883 to open the Southern Exposition. One of three delegates from Louisville who traveled with him on the special train from Washington, Yandell again was mistaken for the president and, from a group of "untutored" Virginians, received stares "like an escaped curiosity from Barnum's circus." John Mason Brown, another of the Louisville hosts, jokingly accused Yandell of trying to pass himself off as the president and suggested that he might be the object of a lawsuit. The doctor quickly surmised that he was the "next best thing" to being president; he was the "Great Presidential Fetcher!"[32]

An articulate lecturer, talented surgeon, dedicated educator, and highly respected citizen, David Yandell was the most progressive and influential member of the university's medical faculty during the postwar era. In the spring of 1895 the university gratefully acknowledged the doctor's services when it placed "upon the brow of this, our greatest son," the highest degree within her power, a Doctor of Laws Degree.[33] Yandell's twentieth-century successors honor his memory with a lectureship that brings to the campus the nation's most prominent and knowledgeable surgeons.

5

EDITOR AND MEDICAL POLITICIAN

FOR MANY of Yandell's associates, teaching was a part-time endeavor that enhanced their professional reputations, provided a handsome remuneration, and required only a few hours of their time each day during the school term. But classroom teaching was a small part of an educator's responsibility, according to Yandell. Medical education only began in the academic atmosphere of the university; Yandell believed that it should continue throughout a doctor's professional life, and he worked unceasingly to make readily available to his practicing colleagues the means to continue their education. For twenty-five years he was the active senior editor of one of the Midwest's leading medical journals, and for nearly a half-century he vigorously participated in and strongly advocated professional societies that both aided in the dissemination of knowledge and worked to improve the profession's standards.

Writing had always been important to the Yandells. Lunsford had edited two medical journals and published more than a hundred articles and treatises. He stressed to his children the importance of conveying one's thoughts with well-chosen words and recording them with a legible hand. Each of the children kept a diary, and before David left for his European studies he was instructed to record his experiences in detail. The publication of his European letters acted as a stimulus for both his medical career and his interest in publishing. Sally and Lunny were also encouraged to develop their writing talents. During his Memphis years Lunny wrote detailed descriptions to his family in Louisville of what he did, saw, and felt, and Susan Yandell read the letters with an editor's thoroughness. Lists of misspelled words, awkward phrases, and grammatical errors were made on each letter and returned to her son. Lunny, in turn, provided much the same sort of service for Sally. The results of this unusual training are evident in the clear, readable letters, articles, and editorials that carried Lunny's name. Whether David's smooth style was developed in the same manner is unknown, but his creative and editorial efforts were enjoyed by thousands of readers for more than a quarter of a century.

In 1870 David established the *American Practitioner*, a 65-to-70-page Louisville publication that appeared monthly until 1886, when it merged with the *Louisville Medical News*. The resulting biweekly *American Practitioner and News* continued under Yandell's editorial guidance until shortly before his death. The *Practitioner* was well received by physicians throughout the Ohio Valley and was given flattering notices by its subscribers, newspapers, and other medical periodicals. Though a professional and literary success, the publication apparently reaped few if any financial benefits for its editors. Subscribers numbered about 2,000 in 1876 and nearly 6,000 by the early 1890s, but the cost of printing the journal usually exceeded its income. The magazine carried numerous notes from the publisher and from its editors urging readers to pay the three-dollar annual subscription fee. It is probable that Yandell absorbed the publication's deficit.

The journal's content included original articles by some of the nation's best-known physicians, reviews of American and European publications, synopses of clinical cases gleaned from other journals or sent to the editors by their subscribers, miscellaneous notes, editorials, and minutes and transactions of local, state, national, and foreign medical organizations. Encompassing every phase of medical knowledge, from the practices of contemporary Chinese doctors to the latest techniques in repairing abdominal wounds, the *Practitioner* gave its readers a generous and well-balanced feast of medical knowledge.

Although he was an infrequent contributor to the section of the journal devoted to original works, some of Yandell's best writing appears here. Much of it had been prepared for addresses and speeches presented to various organizations, but several selections were written especially for the journal. A study of "epidemic convulsions" that characterized the early Kentucky camp meetings was one of his most unusual essays, for it analyzed what has generally been considered an emotional phenomenon as though it was a contagious physical ailment. One cannot help suspecting that Yandell's wit was at work and that his conclusions were written tongue-in-cheek. The article for which he was best known was a classic study of 450 tetanus cases. Appearing in the second volume of the *Practitioner*, the essay was republished and quoted in a variety of journals and medical books. In an era when scientific conclusions usually were drawn from the study of a mere handful of cases, Yandell and one of his associates compiled an unusually large amount of data and compared the various treatments used, concluding that despite the loud acclaim given certain medications, no therapeutic action yet devised was effective against the ravages of tetanus.

A sizable portion of each journal was devoted to reviews. Realizing that practicing physicians could not find time to read every publication that circulated, Yandell reviewed contemporary medical studies that might be valuable additions to his readers' libraries. His reviews usually contained comments on the external appearance of the book, the quality of the woodcuts and engravings, the author's literary style, and the content. An 800-page work on the use of electricity in medicine and surgery was praised for its content but criticized for its lack of brevity. Its bits of grandiloquence, Yandell believed, should have been expunged and left "to sophomores and fourth-of-July orators." Yandell might abhor prolixity or take issue with the author's facts, theories, or conclusions, but usually he diplomatically disagreed with the writer instead of accusing him of being in error. However, his occasional "scathing exposure of wrong doing . . . [caused] many an offending medical brother to regret the publication of an ill written book."[1] An example of his critical reviews is found in the discussion of an 1873 publication on mental hygiene that began with an "incorrect quotation," classified together "the Savior of the World with Solon, Lincoln and Greeley" and concluded with what appeared to be a defense of free love. The editor commented: "The essay indeed is a compound of truth and error, of striking facts and false conclusions, of sound suggestions and absurd, extravagant fancies. . . . the dead flies are small in bulk compared with the ointment, but they are numerous enough to spoil a much larger mass."[2]

Many of Yandell's editorials concerned problems that were common to most of his subscribers. An essay on the decreasing incomes of physicians during the recession of the 1870s reminded his readers that the followers of medicine "can no more escape the calamities which affect other classes than we can fly." Yandell, whose income had declined 50 percent during the panic, suggested that his medical brethren practice economy in everything except their contributions to charity and their purchases of books and medical journals, for they "are to the doctor what capital is to the merchant, stock and seed to the farmer, and prices current to trade. They are simply indispensable."[3]

He also encouraged his readers to support other journals and educational institutions. He urged everyone to write personal appeals to his congressmen to appropriate sufficient money for the completion of the National Medical Library in Washington, and he lauded the publication of the *Index Medicus*, a gigantic undertaking by the surgeon general's office. Lest the *Index* be discontinued for lack of funds, Yandell hoped his readers would subscribe to it, despite its expense (six dollars per year) and its limited value to the average practitioner.

Some of Yandell's editorials touched on problems that still

are of concern to physicians. The medical profession of the late nineteenth century was filled with charlatans and poorly trained physicians who endangered the lives of their patients and harmed the reputation of the profession. Many of Yandell's colleagues advocated the use of the courts to purge the profession of those who threatened it. The laws of every state permitted malpractice suits; yet most state legislatures had passed statutes that hampered medical schools from obtaining dissection subjects, declined to define adequate medical education or restrict the growth of diploma mills, and refused to institute licensing laws. Thus the "saddler, the plasterer, the blacksmith and any other artisan, may declare himself a practitioner of medicine and assume its great responsibilities." Any state that both encouraged and punished quackery and incompetency, Yandell believed, "put out men's eyes, and then punished them for not seeing." Although he wished to rid the profession of those who dishonored it, Yandell had little sympathy for patients whose indiscriminate selection and support of charlatans insulted honest, able, and dedicated physicians. He urged his fellow practitioners to fight for better regulatory laws rather than to encourage malpractice suits as a means of cleansing the profession. The successful suit "stimulates a dozen that have no solid foundation" and causes able men to suffer loss of time, reputation, and income. A malpractice suit, Yandell warned, was a war on the entire profession, not on an erring individual.[4]

Although he seldom hesitated to editorialize on medical controversies, Yandell refrained from entering personal disputes between his colleauges or expressing his political opinions, practices frequently indulged in by other editors of the era. So careful was he to refrain from involving the *Practitioner* in politics that he completely ignored at least one event newsworthy to Kentucky's doctors. In 1879 Louisville physician and sanitarian Luke Pryor Blackburn was elected governor of Kentucky. The *American Practitioner* carried no meı tion of Blackburn's nomination, campaign, or election. Nor were Blackburn's actions as the state's chief executive mentioned, although his aid to the infant State Board of Health and his sanitation reforms in the State Penitentiary at Frankfort were worthy of praise.

The most entertaining selections in the *American Practitioner* were letters written by Yandell and other physicians as they traveled in Europe or in the American West, which in the 1870s and early 1880s was still an area of mystery and romance to Americans living east of the Mississippi. In 1876 Yandell spent several weeks in Texas visiting his brother Willie, acquaintances from his army days, and former students, and while in the Lone Star State he addressed the state's medical society. In a delightful letter to his coeditor, Theophilus Parvin, he described the beauties of the Texas countryside, the friendliness of the people, and the peculiarities of the native foods.

You never ate enchilada, did you Parvin? I hope you never will. You never ate tamallis, did you? Well, don't. An enchilada looks not unlike an ordinary flannelcake, rolled on itself and covered with molasses. The ingredients which go to make it up are pepper, lye-hominy, pepper, onions chopped fine, pepper, grated cheese and pepper. . . . In point of looks the enchilada is, as I have intimated, not uninviting. In point of taste, it is a cross between bicarbonate of soda and capsicum [cayenne pepper], with a good deal of chaw in it. One mouthful would go round an entire family in Louisville.

Yandell concluded that "no man can eat enchilada and tamallis long and remain honest." His published letter received applause from the journal's readers. The Texas Medical Society was delighted with it, and a doctor from Illinois informed Yandell that the highly entertaining and "spicy" selection provided him with some of the "heartiest laughter" he had ever had and suggested that should David ever become weary of practicing medicine he could "undertake the role of traveling correspondent."[5] Perhaps remembering this comment, Yandell wrote for publication accounts of several other interesting trips he took.

A sizable portion of each issue of the *Practitioner* was devoted to reports and transactions of various medical societies.

Yandell was a member of many of these organizations; some of them he had helped to found and had served as an officer. The Kentucky State Medical Society was founded in November 1851; David and his father were among the forty petitioners who requested that the legislature charter the society. By 1880 David was the society's senior member. Throughout his career he served on numerous committees for the KSMS, presented papers on a wide variety of subjects at its annual meetings, and supported the society's endeavors; his father served as one of its presidents and was acting in that capacity when he died in 1878.

Despite his close association with the KSMS David Yandell showed little inclination to be involved in its administrative affairs. Perhaps this was because of the internal strife that characterized the group. Jealousies were always present between faculty and nonfaculty doctors, as they were between rural and urban doctors, specialists and general practitioners. Yandell also expressed some dissatisfaction with many of the long-winded papers presented at the meetings. He believed that individual bedside observations were the topics about which doctors wished to hear; the "rehash of well known opinions and quotations from the horn books are received with rapidly diminishing interest, while the demand for daily observation and clinical experience of the practitioner is steadily on the increase." Yandell warned the KSMS that "medical societies cannot live by papers alone," especially lengthy ones, for "life is too short and science too long to permit time to be wasted."[6]

The medical society with which Yandell was most closely associated was the American Medical Association. Founded in 1847 to uplift the standards of the profession, its annual meetings were attended by delegates representing the nation's hospitals and medical schools and societies; its sessions were devoted to papers and discussions of problems common to the members and relevant to the profession.

Yandell was in Europe when the AMA held its first meeting, but he received considerable notice when a report to the organization on medical literature included comments about his letters. "Dr. [D. W.] Yandell's sprightly letters from Europe seem to have attracted more attention to the *Western Journal of Medicine and Surgery* than have any of its other contents. His portraits [of European physicians] are drawn in spirit, but if certain readers had the hanging of them, some of those placed highest [by Yandell] would come down and their situations be occupied by others which he is disposed to undervalue."[7] The Kentuckian attended his first AMA meeting in 1850 and became a life member of the organization in 1855. His first address to the organization was presented in 1851 in support of clinical teaching in medical schools. Lunsford encouraged his son to involve himself in the association's activities and rejoiced at David's aptitude for "medical politics." He also delighted in his son's speech to the association in 1851 and lauded his 1853 presentation of a paper David and Dr. Gross prepared on "Surgical Operations for the Relief of Malignant Diseases." David apparently attended most of the AMA meetings during the 1850s and made important contacts with the leading physicians of the day.

Yandell's major impact on the AMA came after the Civil War. His position in the Confederate army had introduced him to medical men across the South, and his care of Union prisoners of war, the prestige of his military office, and his reputation for excellence were respected by delegates from North and South. No representatives from the southern states were present at the 1866 AMA meeting, but Yandell was one of several Kentuckians to attend the 1867 meeting in Cincinnati. Delegates to the Queen City meeting, badly split by sectional animosities, spent an inordinate amount of time feuding over whether to nominate a northerner or a southerner for the organization's president. A member of the nominating committee, Yandell urged his fellow delegates to shake hands over the bloody chasm and in a peace-making speech nominated for president his close friend and beloved master, Samuel Gross of Philadelphia. Gross was acceptable to the majority of the delegates, and Yandell was elected one of the organization's three vice-presidents.

Yandell's name was mentioned for the organization's

presidency in 1868 and 1869, but he was unable to attend those meetings to work for his candidacy. He attended the 1871 convention in San Francisco, however, and was elected president of the association, the second Kentuckian to be so honored. Several of his friends had urged him to seek the presidency and had intimated to him that they were working for his nomination. Dr. Gross informed Yandell that he hoped the association would "have the good sense" to elect him, and the orthopedic surgeon Lewis Sayre wrote from New York that he planned to make the journey to vote for his friend. Yandell started for California in doubt, he later said, that he would accept the honor if it were offered, for he believed the position should be bestowed on an older and more experienced man. His reluctance vanished when he realized the strength of his friends' support. When the nominating committee met to choose the president, Yandell was named as their candidate, and the convention unanimously elected him to the highest position the profession could offer to a colleague.[8]

A few weeks after Yandell returned from California, Dr. E. S. Gaillard, the editor of the *Richmond and Louisville Medical Journal* and a faculty member of the Kentucky School of Medicine, accused the newly elected AMA president of frequent falsehoods, persistent literary theft, and conduct unbecoming a medical officer and gentleman in the Confederate States Army. Using his journal as a medium from which to launch his attack, Gaillard informed his readers that Yandell had been an unscholarly student, and had falsely claimed that Daniel Drake had praised his oral examination; that the articles David wrote about his European studies were plagiarized from French and English publications; that he used his influence as army medical director to remove a well-qualified officer from his post as surgeon and replaced him with a member of his own family; and that his entire career with the Confederate army was one of "cock fighting" and overbearing behavior to his subordinates. Henry Watterson, editor of the *Courier-Journal*, immediately printed a refutation of the charges, and Gaillard answered by accusing "Marse Henry" of "propping and pillowing a helpless brother."[9]

In answer to what he labeled Gaillard's "most scurrilous and most mendacious article," Yandell penned a somewhat boastful twenty-page autobiography that refuted some of Gaillard's accusations and ignored others. Yandell regretfully admitted that his student days had not always been well spent, but he denied that Drake (dead for nearly two decades) had criticized his examination and claimed to have a letter from Dr. Gross that substantiated the denial. He labeled groundless the accusation of plagiarism, although large portions of some of the articles he wrote from Europe were copied or paraphrased from foreign publications, and accurately explained his removal as medical director of the Army of the Trans-Mississippi. Pleading innocent to any knowledge that would explain Gaillard's "imbecile attempt to murder the good name of a neighbor, a professional brother and a rival" except the unfortunate loss of his arm during the war, Yandell suggested that perhaps the one-armed Gaillard was to be pitied, for his "mind [is] ill at ease."[10]

Apparently enraged by what he termed Yandell's "endless, ludicrous and fustian piece of advertisement and self glorification," Gaillard continued his diatribes. The row excited considerable interest, but sympathies generally were with Yandell. Several newspapers in the state, whose editors were acquainted with neither Gaillard nor Yandell, noted that the assault was in poor taste and expressed curiosity about Gaillard's motives to "trail his profession into the dust."[11] Most members of the press agreed that although the controversy made delightful copy, Gaillard was ill advised in his attack. If there were any truth in the accusations, he should produce the witnesses he claimed could support them.

The Gaillard-Yandell imbroglio died down in the late summer of 1871, but at the April 1872 meeting of the KSMS Gaillard formally introduced his charges against the AMA president and urged that a committee be appointed to investigate Yandell and that he then be summarily dismissed from the organization. The KSMS presiding officer ruled Gaillard out of order and suggested that the matter be referred to the Louisville College of Physicians and Surgeons, an error in judgment, for the KSMS constitution and bylaws required that all charges made before the group be investigated. Nevertheless, when the state organization showed little interest in acting on Gaillard's request, the entire matter was dropped. Since this was not Gaillard's first attack on an outstanding Louisville doctor, few persons believed the accusations had any truth in them.

Yandell presided over the 1872 AMA convention at Philadelphia, and most of his presidential address to the delegates concerned the state of American medical education, which had received frequent criticism from members of the association.

The profession does not appear to my mind "corrupt and degenerate." I do not believe it is going from bad to worse, and that the people will have to rise in their majesty to stay its downward progress. I cannot see the thing in this light at all, and so I am not ready to appeal to Federal legislation to correct the evils, and certainly should not go to Congress to establish national medical schools. Beyond all controversy there are grave defects in the education of many of our students, and many of our practitioners of medicine. Not a few of them, I am afraid, have a very slight acquaintance with grammar or physical geography, and too many of them know little about etymology and are bad spellers. It is a pity that this is so, and I should be glad to see a different state of things. But are matters in this respect worse than they were in the times of our fathers? Has the case ever been otherwise, do you suppose, in all the history of our profession? At what period was the golden age of medicine, when all who professed it were scholars, and all who aspired to its honors were worthy of them?

For the improvement of basic skills, Yandell urged the creation of better primary and secondary schools; teaching the three R's was not the purpose or responsibility of medical schools.[12]

Replying to comments about the excellence of Italian and German medical schools, whose curricula included such allied sciences as geometry, mineralogy, geology, philosophy, and "principles of design," Yandell noted that while these subjects were of value they had no place in the curriculum of a medical school either, and he suggested that American schools increase their offerings of practical courses so that their students could "drink deep of medicine." He urged an extension of the lecture term, expansion of requirements for graduation, increase in the number of professorships and courses offered, and more teaching by demonstration. The newly inaugurated system at Harvard, whose graduates, "though they may know less of Greek and mathematics, are far better trained than they were formerly in clinical medicine and surgery, and are better qualified to enter upon their duties as practitioners" received Yandell's praise.[13]

The final portion of Yandell's address concerned women physicians, for the question of admitting women to medical schools and medical societies was a subject that had caused heated oratory in and out of AMA meetings. Briefly mentioning the contributions of female physicians during the early Christian era, Yandell concluded that he could find no satisfactory reason why women might not succeed "in some line of our profession" for they were "able nurses." But he had strong doubts that ladies could be surgeons or would become numerous in the profession. Yandell predicted that women's invasion of the male domain, "which is now startling the world by its din, will probably end in no great results" and hoped that women would never embarrass the AMA by requesting membership. "I could not vote for that," Yandell promised. (Thirteen years later, in a graduation address at the first commencement of the short-lived Louisville School of Pharmacy for Women, Yandell gave one reason why he believed women might not be competent physicians and pharmacists: "Silence secures accuracy" and women were never quiet! Wishing the members of his audience good luck in their profession, he warned them against mixing a career and marriage, for "if you require your husbands to broil their own chops, you may expect them to wish at least to bray you in one of your own mortars.")[14]

In September 1876, as part of the medical profession's celebration of the American Centennial, the International Medical Conference met in Philadelphia, and Yandell attended as a representative of the University of Louisville. At the meeting he established friendships with several well-known European physicians, and these relations were strengthened during his 1878 trip to Great Britain. The visit to Europe was undertaken for his health and to "rest from professional labors," but he was kept busy as the guest of numerous medical schools and societies in London and Edinburgh. His personal friends complained: "One can never get a peek at you. Where do you conceal yourself from your friends?"[15] To his brother in Louisville David admitted pleasure in the attention he received. "Whenever I can get close to these swells, they are my meat. I capture all that I am thrown much with. But remember, my boy, this is the kindest and most civilized and most hospitable people in the world and therefore an easy one to hive. . . . *I am getting fat*—for me. I do believe I look five years younger and feel ten otherwise."[16]

Three years later Yandell represented the surgical section of the AMA at the 1881 International Congress in London. Among those who attended were many of Yandell's friends—the pathologist Rudolph Virchow, the bacteriologist Louis Pasteur, the surgeons Thomas Bryant and Joseph Lister, the pharmacologist Thomas Lauder Brunton, and the pathologist Sir James Paget, president of the congress.

Using his 1881 trip to the London congress as an opportunity for a family vacation, David, his wife, and Susie spent several months sightseeing in Scotland and England. Fanny planned their itinerary, and her husband lovingly nicknamed her "the General," comparing her determination to cover every inch of the countryside to that of Sherman as he marched to the sea. Yandell enjoyed their travels and wrote witty letters for the *Practitioner* about their experiences, but he was happiest in the company of other physicians. The June issue of the *British Medical Journal* announced that Yandell, a "great favorite in medical circles here," was receiving warm welcomes from friends who "appreciated his wit and wisdom." The Kentuckian surprised many of his friends with unusual gifts from America. Brunton, whose childhood fantasies had included living as an Indian chief in the American West, was elated with a "much coveted" skin of a grizzly bear from Yandell, and another friend included among his prized possessions wapiti deer antlers Yandell presented for his game room.[17]

Yandell's 1881 trip to Europe was the lengthiest he made to attend a medical conclave, but it was not the last. For another decade he regularly attended meetings of the KSMS, the Mississippi Valley Editors Association, the American Surgical Association, and various Louisville organizations. His interest in the AMA, however, seemed to wane somewhat after 1885. At the 1885 AMA meeting in New Orleans, Yandell was reelected chairman of the organization's surgical section, despite his absence from the conclave, and he was chosen to chair the surgical section of the 1886 International Medical Congress. Most of the other section heads for the congress were also the "eminently scientific men" who had dominated and guided the AMA during its first four decades. But objections voiced by some of the younger members were so loud that a new committee was appointed to select new officers. Several of the AMA section heads resigned in protest.

The new committee met in Chicago. Yandell's positions were reaffirmed, but many of those chosen were young, unknown men. Numerous state medical societies drew up petitions labeling the Chicago group's actions "detrimental to the interest of the medical profession"; signatures of some of the best known physicians of the era—Alfred Stillé, Henry P. Bowditch, William Osler, Samuel Gross, James R. Chadwick, David H. Agnew, Oliver Wendell Holmes, and David Yandell—were on these petitions. The *American Practitioner* reported that the AMA had been "led astray."[18]

Shortly after the Chicago meeting, Yandell, vacationing in New Hampshire, received clippings from the *Courier-Journal* that quoted W. H. Wathen, a Louisville physician serving on the new committee, who claimed credit for convincing anti-Yandell members of the committee to reappoint the surgeon to his former office. Yandell immediately demanded an explanation of Wathen's statement. For several weeks the two men corresponded in polite anger. Resenting anyone either opposing him or claiming to be responsible for reappointing him to a position he had held for many years, Yandell resigned both his chairmanship in the AMA and his appointment to the congress. Wathen chided Yandell for attending only a few AMA meetings and thus robbing the organization of his talents. Yandell's election to the AMA presidency, wrote Wathen, had apparently resulted from ambitious plotting, for he had contributed no scientific papers at its meetings; his premature election to the presidency had gone to his head.

Yandell's election may have resulted from astute campaigning, and it is probable that the honor inflated his ego, but Wathen's other accusations were erroneous. Yandell had attended most of the AMA meetings since the mid 1850s and had delivered several papers on surgery, the most important of which was the one he and Gross prepared for the 1853 meeting.

Despite his resignation from the surgical committee, Yandell retained his membership in the AMA. His last major public speech was delivered to the AMA in 1892. Nevertheless, a new interest did capture much of his time and energy during the 1880s. In 1879 Samuel Gross organized a society of surgeons, which, as the American Surgical Association, held its first annual meeting the following year. Yandell was among the fifty surgeons who attended that meeting, and for more than a decade he served as one of the association's most active members. Like the AMA, the ASA bestowed its presidency upon its outstanding member as an honor, and Yandell was elected to the office in 1889, presiding at the 1890 meeting. His presidential address, "Pioneer Surgery in Kentucky," was his best literary work. Lamenting that the outstanding deeds of many physicians had gone unsung, Yandell lauded four of the commonwealth's early surgeons: Walter Brashear, who performed the first hip-joint amputation; Ephraim McDowell, the father of ovariotomy; Charles McCreary, who performed the first complete extirpation of the clavicle; and Benjamin Dudley, a founder of the medical school at Transylvania and longtime teacher there, who perfected the lithotomy. Comparing these pioneers to the adventurers who settled and tamed the nation's wilderness, Yandell told his audience that they "blazed a path through the unexplored regions of their art" and "devised measures and dealt with issues in advance of their times." His speech also explained why medical history fascinated him and had been incorporated into so many of his lectures and writings. "Let us who are reaping the harvest which they sowed forget not how much we are beholden to these immortal husbandmen. And as we contemplate the shining record of their deeds, let it counsel us to 'bend ourselves to a better future.' Not that we may hope to rival their sublime achievements, but that each in his walk, however humble it may be, may strive to enlarge the sphere of his unselfishness by making surgery the better for his having practiced it."[19]

Realizing the educational value of a small, specialized organization comprised of physicians with similar interests and problems, Yandell founded the Louisville Surgical Society in 1890 and served as its first president. During his few remaining active years he supported the group's endeavors and reported its activities in the *Practitioner and News*. At the society's meetings, and at all others that he attended during his long life, Yandell enjoyed meeting old friends and becoming reacquainted with the many students he had taught. Apparently he had an uncanny memory for faces. The biography of New York surgeon John A. Wyeth tells of a meeting with his mentor at the 1890 meeting of the Mississippi Valley Medical Association.

My old teacher Prof. David Yandell held a reception at his beautiful residence. The crowd soon filled the house and overflowed into a large marquee in the grounds. I had not seen the host since I was graduated in 1869 and several fellow alumni suggested that we play a trick on the dear old surgeon, whom we might have known was not "born in the night time." I took my place in the line filing up to shake his hands. . . . I did not give him my name as I took his hand, and he said, "You have the advantage of me," to which I replied, "Professor, I am Jim Smith, one of your pupils from Breathitt County. . . . In an instant his handsome face lit up and he put his arm around me and said, loud enough to shock everyone about us: "No, you're not. By God, you're John."[20]

Teacher, editor, founder and president of several professional organizations, member and supporter of others, Yandell won praise from physicians and educators on both sides of the Atlantic. In 1883 he was selected as an honorary member of the Medical Society of London and shortly thereafter was named honorary fellow in the London Medical-Chirurgical Society. In 1887 as part of the organization's celebration of its hundredth birthday the College of Physicians and Surgeons of Philadelphia elected ten prominent American physicians to honorary membership. David Yandell was the only Kentuckian so honored.

Postscript

THE HOMES of David Yandell and his neighbors are gone, demolished during the recent urban renewal program. The 700 block of Chestnut, once filled with stately two- and three-story brick homes of the Italianate style, is now occupied by modern office buildings, parking lots, and a vocational school. United Mercantile Agencies owns the site of the Yandell home, and the hushed din of the business world has replaced the exuberant laughter and tears of family and friends who enjoyed the home during the last half of the nineteenth century. Chestnut Street was rather arrogantly referred to by its residents as "the street," and although more palatial homes could be found on Broadway, Chestnut Street residents were sure that their neighborhood was superior to all others. They even goodnaturedly vied with each other as to which block and which side of the street was the best. One of Yandell's neighbors said that he would like to take "a little bit" of Chestnut between Sixth and Seventh streets to heaven with him. David once sidestepped an inquiry about his political preferences with a boast that he was for the United States, for Kentucky, for Louisville, and "for my side of Chestnut Street."[1]

Gone also are those who inhabited the Chestnut Street home—Lunsford, Susan, Lunny, Sally, Willie, Fanny, Susie, Allison, Maria, and David. David's last few years were marred by arteriosclerosis which affected his memory and personality, and in 1896 a stroke destroyed his remaining faculties. For nearly two years his family nursed the empty shell of a man who once charmed presidents and generals with his wit and awed greenhorn medical students with his knowledge and skill. Surrounded by those he loved best, David Yandell died May 2, 1898.

The old medical building in which David, Lunsford, and Lunny taught has disappeared, as have the various other medical schools in Louisville with which the university competed for so many years. The Kentucky School of Medicine, Louisville Medical College, Louisville Hospital College, and Kentucky University Medical Department merged with the University of Louisville's medical department during the first decade of the twentieth century. The commodious stone building belonging to the Louisville Medical College, built in 1890 at First and Chestnut, became the new home of the consolidated school. The university's old building at Eighth and Chestnut was sold to the Louisville school board and was used for another half-century as a public school. Eventually, it too became a victim of urban renewal.

With the consolidation of Louisville's medical schools, the enrollment and income of the university's medical department swelled, but it was unable to provide sufficient facilities for so large a student body. In 1909 representatives of the Carnegie Foundation for the Advancement of Teaching studied and analyzed the university and other medical schools across the nation, and their published review, usually referred to as the Flexner report, indicated grave weaknesses in the nation's medical schools. The report's major criticism of the Louisville school concerned its low entrance requirements (a high school diploma, even one from a two-year school); insufficient laboratory, clinical, and hospital facilities; and unmanageably large classes. "The outlook is not promising," concluded the report.[2]

Prior to the report's publication the university's trustees instituted major changes. They reorganized the school's faculty, improved its physical plant, lengthened its annual sessions, and revamped its entrance requirements to meet the standards suggested by the AMA, the Association of American Medical Colleges, and the Carnegie Foundation. The school survived, and in subsequent years it has developed into a modern institution in which Kentuckians take pride.

In 1970 the University of Louisville School of Medicine moved into a new multimillion-dollar medical center. Were David Yandell to visit this new complex, he undoubtedly would be awed but elated by its modern teaching, clinical, and research facilities. The school that Lunsford Yandell helped found and that David Yandell nurtured and guided through its infancy has come of age.

Notes

Chapter 1

1. Journal of Lunsford Pitts Yandell [n.d.], Yandell Family Papers, The Filson Club, Louisville. The Yandell Papers consist of two collections. The larger one, donated by Malcolm C. Henderson of Berkeley, California, will be cited hereafter as YFP. The smaller collection, a gift from W. R. Wood of Melbourne Beach, Florida, will be cited as YFP-Wood.

2. Ibid.; Susan W. Yandell to Sarah Wendel, Feb. 1, 1831, YFP.

3. Susan W. Yandell to David Wendel, Oct. 28, 1832, YFP.

4. Ibid.; Lunsford Pitts Yandell to Sarah Wendel, Dec. 25, 1832, YFP.

5. Journal of Lunsford Pitts Yandell [n.d.], YFP.

6. *Acts of the General Assembly of the Commonwealth of Kentucky, 1832–1833* (Frankfort, 1833), p. 300; Lunsford Pitts Yandell, *History of the Medical Department of the University of Louisville: An Introductory Lecture* (Louisville, 1853), p. 9.

7. [Lunsford Pitts Yandell], *Narrative of the Dissolution of the Medical Department of Transylvania University* (Nashville, Tenn., 1837), pp. 5, 10.

8. *Lexington Intelligencer*, Apr. 14, 1837; *Louisville Public Advertiser*, Mar. 25, 1837.

9. *Circular Address of the President and Faculty of the Louisville Medical Institute* (Louisville, 1837), p. 4.

10. Lunsford P. Yandell, *History of the Medical Department*, p. 13; Lunsford P. Yandell to Charles Wilkins Short, June 3, 1838, Charles Wilkins Short Collection, The Filson Club, Louisville.

11. David W. Yandell, "Reminiscences of the Teachers of Medicine in the University of Louisville," *Fifty-First Annual Announcement of the University of Louisville* (Louisville, 1887), p. 25.

12. Ibid., p. 28.

13. Ibid.

14. Ibid., p. 26.

15. Thomas B. Greenley, "Reminiscences of the Lives and Character of Some of the Old Time Physicians of Louisville," The Filson Club, Louisville.

16. David Yandell, "Reminiscences of the Teachers of Medicine," pp. 28–29; Daniel Drake, On the Means of Promoting the Intellectual Improvement of the Students and Physicians of the Valley of the Mississippi: An Introductory Lecture (Louisville, 1844), pp. 5, 21; Daniel Drake, An Introductory Discourse to a Course of Lectures on Clinical Medicine and Pathological Anatomy Delivered at the Opening of the New Clinical Amphitheatre of the Louisville Marine Hospital (Louisville, 1840), p. 10.

17. Samuel D. Gross, Autobiography of Samuel D. Gross, M.D., with Sketches of his Contemporaries, ed. by his sons, 2 vols. (Philadelphia, 1887), 1:160; David Yandell, "Reminiscences of the Teachers of Medicine," p. 29.

18. Greenley, "Reminiscences."

19. John Q. Anderson, ed., Louisiana Swamp Doctor: The Writings of Henry Clay Lewis, Alias "Madison Tensas, M.D." (Baton Rouge, La., 1962), pp. 164–65.

20. David W. Yandell, Reply to the Attack of Dr. E. S. Gaillard (Louisville, 1871), p. 4.

21. Greenley, "Reminiscences."

22. Frances C. Yandell, biography of David W. Yandell, private collection of W. R. Wood, Melbourne Beach, Fla.

Chapter 2

1. Emmett F. Horine, "History of the Louisville Medical Institute," The Filson Club History Quarterly 7 (July 1933):147.

2. Journal of David Yandell, p. 1, YFP-Wood.

3. Ibid., pp. 10, 14.

4. Ibid., p. 24.

5. David W. Yandell, "Clinical Instruction in the London and Paris Hospitals," Western Journal of Medicine and Surgery, 3d ser. 2 (Nov. 1849):393.

6. David W. Yandell, "Notes on the Medical Men and Medical Matters of London and Paris," Western Journal of Medicine and Surgery, n.s. 6 (Aug. 1846):130.

7. David W. Yandell, letter to the Louisville Journal, written May

21, 1846, undated newspaper clipping in Yandell Folder, WPA File, Kornhauser Health Sciences Library, University of Louisville.

8. Ibid., written July 15, 1846.

9. David W. Yandell, "Foreign Correspondence," *Western Journal of Medicine and Surgery*, n.s. 6(Nov. 1846):397.

10. David Yandell, "Clinical Instruction," p. 397.

11. Ibid., p. 398.

12. Ibid., p. 393.

13. Lunsford P. Yandell to Susan Yandell, Aug. 28, Sept. 3, Sept. 5, 1850, YFP.

14. Lunsford P. Yandell to Susan Yandell, May 12, 1850, YFP; Susan Yandell to Lunsford P. Yandell, Jr., Aug. 3, 1859, YFP; Susan Yandell to Lunsford P. Yandell, Mar. 28, Apr. 2, Apr. 8, 1851, YFP.

15. Susan Yandell to Lunsford P. Yandell, Apr. 4, 1851, YFP; Herschel Gower, *Pen and Sword: The Life and Journals of Randal W. McGavock* (Nashville, Tenn., 1959), p. 173.

16. Susan Yandell to Lunsford P. Yandell, May 4, 1851, YFP; Lunsford P. Yandell to Susan Yandell, May 14, 1853, YFP.

17. Susan Yandell to Lunsford P. Yandell, Jr., May 7, 1859, YFP.

18. Ibid.

19. Minutes of the Medical Faculty of the University of Louisville, May 1859, Kornhauser Health Sciences Library.

20. Susan Yandell to Lunsford P. Yandell, Jr., Jan. 1, 1859, YFP; Lunsford P. Yandell, Jr., to Sally Yandell, July 19, 1860, YFP.

21. Lunsford P. Yandell, Jr., to Lunsford P. Yandell, Apr. 21, 1859, YFP; Lunsford P. Yandell to Susan Yandell, June 2, 1859, YFP.

22. Journal of Lunsford P. Yandell [n.d.], YFP.

23. William Yandell to Sally Yandell, Jan. 25, 1861, YFP.

24. Diary of William Yandell, Aug. 15, 1852, YFP.

Chapter 3

1. Diary of Lunsford P. Yandell, Apr. 12, 1861, YFP.

2. Lunsford P. Yandell, Jr., to Lunsford P. Yandell, Apr. 12, 1861; "Notes and Queries," *American Practitioner* 31 (May 1885):172. The latter contains a memorial address on the life of Lunsford Pitts Yandell, Jr.

3. Minutes of the Medical Faculty, Sept. 20, 1861; diary of Lunsford P. Yandell [Sept. 1861], YFP.

4. "Surgeon" was the rank granted to a graduate medical doctor in

the regular army. The word also was loosely used to refer to anyone who practiced medicine.

5. William Preston Johnston, *Life of Albert Sidney Johnston* (New York, 1879), p. 360.

6. Jacob Fraise Richard, *The Florence Nightingale of the Southern Army* (New York, 1914), p. 39.

7. Diary of Josie Underwood Nazro, Dec. 3, 1861, typescript, Kentucky Library, Western Kentucky University.

8. D. W. Yandell to W. W. Mackall, Oct. 27, 1861, Papers relating to David W. Yandell, General and Staff Officers' File, Old Army Section, National Archives, Washington, D.C. The collection will hereafter be cited as YP-Nat. Archives.

9. *House Journal of the First Session of the 34th General Assembly of the State of Tennessee* (Nashville, 1957), p. 208; D. W. Yandell to A. S. Johnston, Nov. 9, 1861, YP-Nat. Archives.

10. W. G. Stevenson, *Thirteen Months in the Confederate Army* (New York, 1864), p. 102.

11. D. W. Yandell to W. W. Mackall, Jan. 11, 1862, YP-Nat. Archives.

12. Ibid., Nov. 23, 1861.

13. Ibid., Dec. 1, 1861.

14. D. W. Yandell to Samuel Hollingsworth Stout, Aug. 18, 1862, Samuel Hollingsworth Stout Manuscripts, William Perkins Library, Duke University; "A Confederate," *The Gray Jackets and How They Lived and Died for Dixie* (Richmond, Va., 1867), pp. 73–74.

15. D. W. Yandell to Lunsford P. Yandell, Dec. 22, 1861, YFP.

16. Undated circular from D. W. Yandell, Andrew J. Foard's letter book, Military Collection, Virginia State Library, Richmond, Va., hereafter cited as Foard's letter book.

17. Charles R. Mott, Jr., ed., "War Journal of a Confederate Officer," *Tennessee History Quarterly* 5(Sept. 1946):238.

18. A. W. Barnett to Wirt Adams, Jan. 11, 1862, Foard's letter book; D. W. Yandell to A. W. Barnett, Jan. 18, 1862, ibid.

19. Kate Cummings, *A Journal of Hospital Life in the Confederate Army from the Battle of Shiloh to the End of the War* (Louisville, 1866), p. 53.

20. Ibid., pp. 12–13.

21. D. W. Yandell to William P. Johnston, Nov. 11, 1877, Mrs. Mason Barrett Collection of Johnston Papers, Howard-Tilton Library, Tulane University, hereafter cited as Johnston Papers.

22. F. E. Daniel, *Recollections of a Rebel Surgeon* (Austin, Tex., 1899), p. 53.

23. D. W. Yandell to William P. Johnston, Nov. 8, 1862, Johnston Papers.

24. Basil W. Duke, *Reminiscences of Basil W. Duke, C.S.A.* (Garden City, N.Y., 1911), pp. 503–4.

25. Ibid., p. 505.

26. *The War of the Rebellion: A Compilation of the Official Records of the Union and Confederate Armies*, 128 vols. (Washington, D.C., 1880–1901), ser. 1, vol. 20, pt. 1, p. 779, hereafter cited as *Official Records*.

27. Jefferson Davis to Joseph E. Johnston, Aug. 24, 1863, in Dunbar Rowland, *Jefferson Davis, Constitutionalist*, 10 vols. (Jackson, Miss., 1923), 6:1; David W. Yandell, *Reply to the Attack of Dr. E. S. Gaillard* (Louisville, 1871), p. 12.

28. Preston B. Scott to D. W. Yandell, Dec. 5, 1863, YFP-Wood.

29. D. W. Yandell to Lunsford P. Yandell, Dec. 22, 1861, YFP; Frances C. Yandell to Lunsford P. Yandell, Mar. 22, 1862, YFP.

30. Lunsford P. Yandell, Jr., to Lunsford P. Yandell, June 12, 1864, YFP.

31. *Official Records*, ser. 1, vol. 34, pt. 1, p. 569; F. Sanger to D. W. Yandell, June 16, 1864, YFP-Wood.

32. J. W. Berrien to John M. Haden, May 19, 1864, YP-Nat. Archives.

33. E. Kirby Smith to S. Cooper, Oct. 10, 1864, YP-Nat. Archives.

34. Diary of Sally Yandell [n.d.], YFP; D. W. Yandell to ———— McLean, May 31, 1864, Eldridge Collection, Huntington Library, San Marino, Calif.; quoted in Sally Yandell, "A Girl's Experiences in the Confederacy," pp. 17–18, typescript, collection of W. R. Wood.

35. J. G. Walker to D. W. Yandell, Oct. 2, 1864, in *Official Records*, ser. 2, vol. 2, p. 563.

36. Although Yandell's official surrender returned him to civilian status and the amnesty acts of 1868 and 1872 pardoned him for his war activities, it was only recently that a curious charge of "treason against Kentucky" was withdrawn. Six months after the Confederates evacuated Bowling Green, a Warren County grand jury named many officers of the Army of the West, including Yandell, as traitors to the commonwealth—a charge of questionable legality since states do not have treason laws. This indictment was brought to the attention of the local court in 1957, and the court withdrew it. See *Common-*

111

wealth v. *Simon B. Buckner and Others*, Aug. 21, 1862, Warren County Court Records, Kentucky Library, Western Kentucky University; and *Park City Daily News*, Jan. 6, 1958.

37. Quoted in Sally Yandell, "A Girl's Experience," p. 18, Collection of W. R. Wood.

38. Ibid., p. 6.

39. Ibid., p. 9; diary of Sally Yandell, Mar. 18, 1865, YFP.

40. William Yandell to Sally Yandell, Feb. 20, 1864, YFP.

41. "Notes and Queries," *American Practitioner* 31(May 1885): 172; Sally Yandell, "A Girl's Experiences," p. 18, Collection of W. R. Wood.

42. Frances Yandell, biography of David W. Yandell, Collection of W. R. Wood; Benjamin S. Ewell to D. W. Yandell, May 1, 1866, YFP-Wood.

43. *Courier-Journal*, Sept. 19, 1865.

Chapter 4

1. David W. Yandell, *Reply to the Attack of Dr. E. S. Gaillard* (Louisville, 1871), p. 15.

2. Sally Yandell to Lunsford P. Yandell, Jr., Aug. 7 and Sept. 4, 1867, YFP.

3. Last will and testament of David W. Yandell, Will Book 21, p. 661, Jefferson County Court House, Louisville.

4. Susan Yandell to Lunsford P. Yandell, Jr., Apr. 9, 1859, YFP.

5. Flexner's father was a peddler-turned-merchant. The Flexner sons Simon (1889 graduate of the University of Louisville School of Medicine) and Abraham both became leaders in the field of medical education.

6. Henry Heuser, "Some of My Recollections of Dr. David Wendel Yandell," typescript, The Filson Club.

7. W. B. Doherty, "The Old College of Physicians and Surgeons," *Journal of the Kentucky Medical Association* 29(Aug. 1931):443–44.

8. Undated *Louisville Times* clipping, Collection of W. R. Wood.

9. David W. Yandell, "A Discourse on the Life and Character of Dr. Lewis Rogers," *American Practitioner* 12(Nov. 1875):274, 278.

10. David W. Yandell, *The Progress of Medicine:An Introductory Lecture* (Louisville, 1869), pp. 10, 19.

11. H. A. Cottell, "The Life and Character of Prof. David W. Yandell, M.D., LL.D.," *American Practitioner and News* 27 (Apr. 15, 1899):300–301.

112

12. David W. Yandell, "On Some New Remedies," *Louisville Medical News* 2(Dec. 2, 1876):270.

13. David W. Yandell, "On Sebaceous Tumors," ibid., 2 (Dec. 9, 1876):284.

14. Cottell, "David W. Yandell," p. 301.

15. Frances Yandell, biography of David W. Yandell, Collection of W. R. Wood.

16. John A. Wyeth, *With Sword and Scalpel: The Autobiography of a Soldier and Surgeon* (New York, 1914), p. 329.

17. Faculty minutes, p. 178.

18. David W. Yandell, *Address before the American Medical Association, Philadelphia, May 7, 1872* (Louisville, 1872), pp. 17–18.

19. "Annual Report of the Eastern Dispensary," *Louisville Municipal Reports, 1869* (Louisville, 1870), p. 4.

20. Faculty minutes, Dec. 17 and 26, 1867.

21. Lunsford P. Yandell, Jr., to Sally Yandell, Feb. 1861, YFP.

22. Faculty minutes, June 22, 1869.

23. Ibid., June 19, 1871.

24. *Courier-Journal*, July 3, 1874.

25. Faculty minutes, June 22 and 23, 1884.

26. Minutes of the Board of Trustees of the University of Louisville [n.d.], microfilm, University Archives, University of Louisville.

27. Minutes of the Board of School Trustees, Book D, 1866–1878, p. 237, Louisville Board of Education.

28. Faculty minutes, June 19, 1871, and Sept. 10, 1873.

29. Ibid., May 12, 1881.

30. Tom Wallace, "Henry Watterson: A Man of Salient Character," *The Filson Club History Quarterly* 23(Oct. 1949):226.

31. *Louisville Times*, July 28, 1949.

32. *Courier-Journal*, July 31, 1883.

33. Speech delivered at the annual commencement, March 16, 1895, typescript, Collection of W. R. Wood.

Chapter 5

1. "Reviews," *American Practitioner* 11(Apr. 1875):217; Samuel D. Gross, *Autobiography of Samuel D. Gross, M.D., with Sketches of his Contemporaries*, ed. by his sons, 2 vols. (Philadelphia, 1887), 2:6.

2. "Reviews," *American Practitioner* 9(Jan. 1874):95.

3. "Notes and Queries," *American Practitioner* 19(Jan. 1879):68, 70.

4. Ibid., 15 (Jan. 1877):57, 59.

5. Ibid., 13 (May 1876):331; R. E. Hamett to D. W. Yandell, May 6, 1876, YFP-Wood.

6. "Kentucky State Medical Transactions," *American Practitioner* 30(Aug. 1884):245; ibid., 24(Aug. 1881):124.

7. *Transactions of the American Medical Association* (Washington, 1847), pp. 268–69.

8. David W. Yandell, *Reply to the Attack of Dr. E. S. Gaillard* (Louisville, 1871), p. 17.

9. Undated newspaper clipping, Yandell Folder, WPA File, Kornhauser Health Sciences Library.

10. Yandell, *Reply to Gaillard*, pp. 1, 19, 20.

11. Undated newspaper clipping, Yandell Folder, WPA File; William Preston to Henry Watterson, June 10, 1871, YFP-Wood.

12. David W. Yandell, *Address before the American Medical Association, Philadelphia, May 7, 1872* (Louisville, 1872), pp. 10–11.

13. Ibid., p. 23.

14. Ibid., pp. 27–28; David W. Yandell, "Female Pharmacists," *American Practitioner* 30 (Dec. 1884):324, 326.

15. Benjamin Helm Bristow to E. A. Noyes, Mar. 27, 1878, YFP-Wood; J. Milner Fothergill to D. W. Yandell, June 27, 1878, YFP-Wood.

16. D. W. Yandell to Lunsford P. Yandell, Jr., June 8, 1878, YFP-Wood.

17. *British Medical Journal* 1(June 18, 1881):972; Thomas Lauder Brunton to D. W. Yandell [1881], YFP-Wood.

18. "Notes and Queries," *American Practitioner* 32(Sept. 1885):134.

19. David W. Yandell, "Pioneer Surgery in Kentucky," *American Practitioner and News* 10 (July 5, 1891):10.

20. John A. Wyeth, *With Sword and Scalpel: The Autobiography of a Soldier and Surgeon* (New York, 1914), pp. 389–90.

Postscript

1. *Louisville Times*, Oct. 8, 1953.

2. Abraham Flexner, *Medical Education in the United States and Canada: A Report of the Carnegie Foundation for the Advancement of Teaching* (New York, 1910), p. 231.

A Note to Readers

HISTORICAL NARRATIVES traditionally have concentrated on political and military history to the exclusion of medical affairs, for politicians are usually more colorful than physicians and wars are more exciting than diseases. However, for those interested in medical history, several general works not listed in the notes of this study are recommended.

The Works Progress Administration, *Medicine and Its Development in Kentucky* (Louisville, 1940), and the recent Bicentennial contribution, John E. Ellis, *Medicine in Kentucky* (Lexington, Ky., 1977), are the only known general medical histories of the commonwealth. An interesting account of medicine in antebellum Kentucky is found in Madge E. Pickard and R. Carlyle Buley, *The Midwest Pioneer, His Ills, Cures and Doctors* (Crawfordsville, Ind., 1945). Two histories of the state's nineteenth-century medical schools—Robert Peter, *The History of the Medical Department of Transylvania University*, ed. Johanna Peter, Filson Club Publication no. 20 (Louisville, 1905), and Works Progress Administration, *A Centennial History of the University of Louisville* (Louisville, 1939)—provide additional insight into Kentucky's medical history.

The problems that characterized Civil War medicine are found in Horace H. Cunningham, *Doctors in Gray: The Confederate Medical Service* (Baton Rouge, La., 1958), and George W. Adams, *Doctors in Blue: The Medical History of the Union Army in the Civil War* (New York, 1952). Military histories of the Civil War are almost limitless. Among the secondary works used for this study were James G. Randall and David Donald, *The Civil War and Reconstruction*, 2d ed. rev. (Lexington, Mass., 1969); E. M. Coulter, *Civil War and Readjustment in Kentucky* (Chapel Hill, N.C., 1926); and Lowell H. Harrison, *The Civil War in Kentucky* (Lexington, Ky., 1975).

Numerous studies of medicine and medical education have been written in the last few decades, although a definitive work on medicine in the United States has not appeared. Among the best general histories are Frances R. Packard, *History of Medicine in the United States*, 2 vols. (New York, 1931); John Duffey, *The Healers* (New York, 1976); William G. Rothstein, *American Physicians of the Nineteenth Century, from Sect to Science* (Baltimore, Md., 1972); William F. Norwood, *Medical Education in the United States before the Civil War* (Philadelphia, 1944); Joseph Kett, *Formation of the American Medical Profession* (New Haven, Conn., 1963); and Morris Fishbein, *History of the American Medical Association 1847–1947* (Philadelphia, 1947).